# What's GOOD About TODAY?

A Purpose-Driven Life

Christopher Cochran

© **Copyright 2024 - All rights reserved.**

The content contained within this book may not be reproduced, duplicated or transmitted without direct written permission from the author or the publisher.

Under no circumstances will any blame or legal responsibility be held against the publisher, or author, for any damages, reparation, or monetary loss due to the information contained within this book, either directly or indirectly.

Legal Notice:

This book is copyright protected. It is only for personal use. You cannot amend, distribute, sell, use, quote or paraphrase any part, or the content within this book, without the consent of the author or publisher.

Disclaimer Notice:

Please note the information contained within this document is for educational and entertainment purposes only. All effort has been executed to present accurate, up to date, reliable, complete information. No warranties of any kind are declared or implied. Readers acknowledge that the author is not engaged in the rendering of legal, financial, medical or professional advice. The content within this book has been derived from various sources. Please consult a licensed professional before attempting any techniques outlined in this book.

By reading this document, the reader agrees that under no circumstances is the author responsible for any losses, direct or indirect, that are incurred as a result of the use of the information contained within this document, including, but not limited to, errors, omissions, or inaccuracies.

# Table of Contents

INTRODUCTION .................................................................................... 1
    AUTHOR CREDENTIALS ............................................................................ 2

**CHAPTER 1: A RADIANT SPIRIT** ........................................................... 5
    CHRISTIAN'S RADIANT SPIRIT ................................................................... 6
    INNOCENCE AND BEGINNINGS ................................................................ 7
    FACED WITH THE UNTHINKABLE ............................................................. 18
        *A Mother's Journal* ........................................................................ *18*
        *Rachael's Journal* .......................................................................... *26*
    CONCLUDING THOUGHTS: INSPIRED BY CHRISTIAN ................................. 29

**CHAPTER 2: THE CHANGE** ................................................................. 31
    THE QUESTION THAT CHANGED EVERYTHING ......................................... 31
    THE ART OF PAUSING ........................................................................... 35
        *Cholangiocarcinoma: Bile Duct Cancer* ........................................ *36*
    THE BRIGHT SIDE: HARNESSING POSITIVE POWER ................................. 39
        *CaringBridge Journal Entries* ........................................................ *40*
    EMBRACING SPIRITUALITY .................................................................... 55
        *Navigating Loss Faithfully* ............................................................. *56*
    CONCLUDING THOUGHTS: INSPIRED BY CHRISTIAN ................................. 58

**CHAPTER 3: CHRISTIAN'S TAO** .......................................................... 59
    THE TAOIST WAY: GOING WITH THE FLOW ........................................... 59
    LEARNING FROM ALL WALKS OF LIFE ..................................................... 61
    LOVE, COURAGE, KINDNESS ................................................................. 64
        *Christian's Favorites* ..................................................................... *65*
    CONCLUDING THOUGHTS ...................................................................... 68
    CONCLUDING THOUGHTS: INSPIRED BY CHRISTIAN ................................. 69

**CHAPTER 4: THE ROLE MODEL** .......................................................... 71
    A ROLE MODEL FOR MANY ................................................................... 71
    LESSONS LEARNED ............................................................................... 75
    EMBRACING THE PRESENT .................................................................... 81
    CONCLUDING THOUGHTS: INSPIRED BY CHRISTIAN ................................. 84

**CHAPTER 5: A FATHER'S VIEW** .......................................................... 85
    MY PATERNAL OBSERVATIONS .............................................................. 86

*Christian and Rachael* ................................................................. *90*
FROM HELPLESSNESS TO LIGHT ............................................................. 92
APPRECIATING SMALL THINGS ............................................................... 99
THOUGHTS: INSPIRED BY CHRISTIAN ..................................................... 106

## CHAPTER 6: 8,508 DAYS ............................................................... 107

CHRISTIAN'S 8,508-DAY LIFE PATH ..................................................... 107
  *A Mother's Impressions* ............................................................ *108*
  *Online Media Impressions* .......................................................... *117*
LIVING A MEANINGFUL LIFE ................................................................ 118
A LEGACY OF RESILIENCE ................................................................... 121
CONCLUDING THOUGHTS: INSPIRED BY CHRISTIAN ................................... 121

## CHAPTER 7: BETWEEN HOPE AND ACCEPTANCE ......................... 123

GRIEVING AS A FAMILY ...................................................................... 123
CHRISTIAN'S WISH ............................................................................. 126
THE FINAL GOODBYE .......................................................................... 129
  *The Eulogy* ................................................................................ *133*
CONCLUDING THOUGHTS: INSPIRED BY CHRISTIAN ................................... 141

## CHAPTER 8: A LASTING IMPACT ................................................. 143

CHRISTIAN'S LASTING LEGACY ............................................................ 143
CULTIVATING A GRATITUDE MINDSET .................................................... 145
THE PATH OF POSITIVITY .................................................................... 147
  *Touched by Christian's Legacy* .................................................... *148*

## CONCLUSION ................................................................................. 165

## REFERENCES ................................................................................ 169

# Introduction

*Losing Christian feels like a loss of breath that weighs on us every single day.* –
Christopher

These words are for Christian. You have touched our lives. May our words now touch as you have.

This book represents our captivating journey through Christian's short, though extraordinary life, spanning a mere 23 years. In that time, he fearlessly confronted terminal cancer with his unwavering spirit, boundless wisdom, and a deep appreciation for the beauty of diverse spiritual perspectives. I hope to offer some insight to guide your questions, assist with overcoming challenges, cultivate resilience, and foster a sense of acceptance. I would like to help you embrace positivity, navigate grief, and find beauty in every moment—like my son used to do. He has been an inspiration to our family and many others since he entered this broken world—and after he passed to another one.

There is something good about each day.

Not even in the most difficult times during his battle with cancer did Christian ever complain about his diagnosis or dwell on what was going to be his eventual demise. I believe this demonstrates his positive resilience in the face of his terminal illness. He remained positive, charismatic, and even funny, leaving a lasting effect on everyone he touched.

Christian was one of the most joyful, energetic, and positive people you could ever hope to know. His brilliant, beaming smile and boundless energy were a source of joy and comfort to all whose paths he crossed. He was empathetic, loving, and inclusive to everyone he encountered.

On August 26th, 2020, Christian was diagnosed with a rare cancer of the liver: cholangiocarcinoma. When we told him how sorry we were, as his parents, that he had to have this awful disease, he replied: "It's okay, because if it were not me, then it would be someone else that would have to endure this struggle."

Eventually, Christian's cancer spread to his bones. Much of his spine, his femur, his hip, and his shoulders became involved. Amazingly, he never complained. He would often ask us all, w*hat's good about today?* It was his daily reminder that we had to focus on everything good within each day and make the very most of it.

When reading through the great many testimonials and letters that surged in after his passing, we cannot deny the legacy that Christian left in this world. People from all cultures, spiritualities, walks of life, ages, and gender identities keep pouring in their blessings and gratitude—even those who had only had brief encounters with Christian.

As a family, we remain humbled by his profound influence in our lives. The journey with him through the most challenging times in the final months of his short life was not easy. But through his unique approach to living a purposeful life—devoid of complaints, and filled with gratitude and joy—we are honored to say that he blessed us with his presence.

## Author Credentials

At the core of who I am lie the roles of father, husband, and friend. These purposes have profoundly shaped my journey and are at the heart of this book. This deeply personal work is inspired by my son Christian, who courageously fought his battle with cancer. Christian's extraordinary perspective on life is exemplified by his daily question, *What's good about today?* It taught us to embrace each day with positivity. His legacy of hope and resilience is a precious gift that I am committed to sharing with the world.

Professionally, my journey spans more than three decades, during which time I've held pivotal roles in sales, marketing, operations, and P&L management within large public companies. As the founder and CEO of BluChip Solutions, I have steered the company to become a leader in workforce management solutions, serving a diverse range of industries.

My position on the board of directors at Coeptis Therapeutics Holdings, Inc. further intertwines my personal experiences with my professional endeavors, as we work to develop advanced cancer therapies. My involvement with *What's GOOD About TODAY?*, a nonprofit organization born from Christian's enduring spirit, is a testament to my dedication to spreading kindness and generosity.

It's my belief that my career, marked by guiding companies through significant growth and championing impactful organizations, reflects a deep-seated commitment to leaving a positive mark on both the business world and the broader community. In *What's GOOD About TODAY?*, I weave together these varied strands of my life, crafting a narrative that I hope speaks to resilience in both professional and personal realms.

This book is more than a memoir; it's a call to embrace each day with joy and gratitude, a tribute to Christian's indomitable spirit, and a guide for others to find light in their own lives.

# Chapter 1:

# A Radiant Spirit

*But I have three precious things which I prize and hold fast. The first is gentleness; the second is economy; and the third is shrinking from taking precedence of others. –*
Lao Tzu

They say that time is fleeting.

Christian was born on May 17th, 1998. From his first encounter with this world, his radiant being touched everyone it came in contact with. Back when he started going to school, I remember learning how to be a father along the way. As was the custom, on the first day of school, the neighborhood would gather to see all the kids off on the school bus. It was always a momentous event with all the kids scurrying around to get the best seat and not be the last to board. Not for Christian: He would patiently wait and let everyone get on the bus while making sure that his friends were okay. He would even let the shy ones on before him, just to give them a confidence nudge. At that tender elementary school age, he instinctively radiated his gentle nature and kindness.

This would happen at social events as well. At sports gatherings and birthday parties, he would be the embodiment of tranquility amid the fun. He was so comfortable in his own skin and being around people, instinctively checking that his siblings were happy and that no one was sad, and gracefully and humbly accepting awards without much fanfare. His younger sister and brother, Kate and Nicholas, shared countless memorable moments with him during a happy childhood and youth. Life at home was filled with playful moments in the pool during summer and fun in the snow during winter.

Festive days and vacations were always cherished and celebrated in a spirit of togetherness. I specifically remember how young Christian loved Christmas and the moments of opening gifts and playing with his new toys with such delight and gratitude. He often wanted to share his toys with his friends and would even check with us to get our approval.

The last vacation we had together, six months before his fatal diagnosis, was spent together as a family over the Christmas season in the splendor of the Grand Canyon. We had a wonderful time together. Christian and his siblings were bonding deeply during this time, enjoying each other's company by sharing stories and making each other laugh. On Christmas morning, Christian and Danielle both woke up early to hike the Bright Angel Trail and watch the sunrise. They loved doing things in nature together, relishing the quiet, the beauty of nature, and the feeling of peace while observing the beauty of the world God created. Little did we know that soon our lives would change irrevocably—and our sense of loss would be as immense as those divisions between the facing cliffs of that canyon.

## Christian's Radiant Spirit

A life lasting only 8,508 days redefines the value of time when we talk about living. I wonder how many of us can say that every day of our lives was lived mindfully and valued for its precious cosmic glimpse in time. How often do we only realize this when it is too late and we are left with regrets and dissatisfaction?

Many cancer patients say how futile it becomes to think about material assets: the big car, the best home, a successful career. Instead, they all encourage the rest of us to become more mindful and focused on the present moment and to cherish the imperceptible things more. They say how they changed their perspectives from focusing on *things* to focusing on *moments* and *people*. Does it really require a terminal illness to make the rest of us aware of this?

Christian's narrative made me aware of how a beacon of light in a darkened world can become a source of hope. Witnessing his journey in this life made me realize how every moment counts. His struggle with cancer made me aware of the profound relevance of time on my own journey. It stopped me in my tracks and made me reassess my aspirations and pursuits. He made me see that every day can be filled with boundless joy and can be valued for what it offers. His story underscored the essence of human connection.

Just the other day, on one of those challenging blue days that inevitably cross our lives, someone suggested that I write a note of something that made my week worthwhile at the end of every week for one year. And then at the end of the year, I should read through all these notes again to see how much positivity filled my year and then take that feeling with me into the next year. It's called practicing positive self-reflection. Such little acts of daily gratitude will surely radiate a ripple effect on our loved ones. Even if they merely make us smile more and complain less.

The qualities that made Christian stand out were his charisma, kindness, incredible sense of humor, and positivity. His compassion for others and his magnetic personality drew people to him and helped him forge deep connections. Christian was a remarkable individual whose grit and resilience defied all the challenges he faced. He approached living with enthusiasm and a vibrant spirit. To him, every day had something good to offer, and he lived his mantra until his last moment with his family. His example was so powerful that it left a lasting legacy rippling through society for years to come.

## Innocence and Beginnings

My incredible journey started when I met Danielle.

She and I crossed paths when I was just 16 and she was 17. We had a casual introduction in high school through mutual friends, exchanging nothing more than a few passing words like "hi" or "hello." At the time, Danielle was a junior while I was a freshman. She was considered an upperclassman, and I was a young, wide-eyed freshman navigating the halls of high school. Both of us distinctly remember the moment we met at a party. As we passed each other on the stairs, there was a flicker of connection. Our eyes caught one another's and for that moment—for both of us—time paused. Little did we know that that encounter would shape our lives in ways we couldn't have imagined.

It's hard to fathom that as teenagers, we could feel such a deep connection so early on. The day after the party, Danielle surprised me by showing up at my house to ask me to go to a movie. Unfortunately, I wasn't home at the time, but she left a message on a paper plate with my younger brother. I remember him eagerly handing me the plate saying, "This girl came by looking for you, and she was driving a white Mercedes. You must go out with her!" Of course, my 10-year-old brother was captivated by the car, but it was the name Danielle that caught *my* attention. I could only think of one Danielle, and she was an upperclassman. I couldn't fathom why she would be interested in me. She was popular, stunningly beautiful, and yes... she drove a Mercedes 280 SEL.

After a moment of contemplation, I mustered up the courage to call her from the push-button phone in my dad's office. I needed complete silence for this momentous call. As I dialed her number, my heart raced with anticipation. She answered, and after a brief conversation, she asked me if I wanted to go to the movies with her. She even had two free tickets to the movie theater. I thought, "Why not?" At that moment, I had completely forgotten about my current girlfriend, who happened to be away on vacation with her parents. Strangely, I wasn't worried about the potential consequences of that. Deep down, I knew that Danielle was someone special and I was determined to find out why. As we spent more time together, I quickly discovered why I was so drawn to Danielle. She possessed an incredible sweetness, kindness, and a great sense of humor. Not to mention, she was undeniably adorable.

We became an inseparable couple, even as I attended the University of Tennessee, while she went to the University of Pittsburgh. Despite the distance, our love remained strong and unwavering. Early on, we both knew that we wanted to build a family together, rooted in the profound love and passion we shared.

After graduating from college, we reconnected and embarked on our journey through life together. We got engaged a year after graduating and tied the knot a year later. During those blissful times, we often discussed our future and the wonderful life we envisioned for ourselves. It was the epitome of the American Dream. We had a joyous engagement and stunning wedding in Danielle's hometown of Meadville, PA.

Throughout our discussions, one topic that always resonated with us was starting a family. We knew it was our destiny to become parents. Two years after our wedding, we were blissfully pregnant with our first child, Christian. We had already decided on the name "Christian" early on. While a few other names crossed our minds, we both knew deep in our hearts that it was meant to be Christian. The name held so much significance, and we believed this child was destined for something extraordinary. It was my wife's dream to have a boy with big brown eyes and that's exactly what was given to us.

The birth was challenging for Danielle, but the moment I laid eyes on Christian's scrunched-up face, all my worries vanished. He was a true beauty, and I was overcome with awe. As Christian grew into a toddler, it became evident that he was no ordinary child. He possessed an incredible intellect, speaking before his first birthday and constructing sentences before 15 months. But it wasn't just his intelligence that set him apart; it was his extraordinary empathy for others that he possessed that never failed to impress. Even at such a young age, he could sense when someone was in pain or feeling unwell. It was truly remarkable. When Danielle wasn't feeling her best or struggling with the challenges of being a new mom, this 15-month-old Christian would offer words of reassurance, saying, "You're okay, you're so precious," as he gently stroked her head to comfort her. Christian carried this exceptional trait with him throughout his life, incorporating it into his daily interactions as a toddler, young child, preteen, teenager, and into his young adult life. He never wavered from his love and compassion for others. He would even call himself, "Mr. Comfort" during his upper elementary school years when family members were sick or sad. He took care of us.

Christian's charm and early inclination as a performer began as a toddler. He would often stand on our living room coffee table and dance, sing, and perform theater. He felt at ease interacting with others from a young age, entertaining them and bringing smiles and laughter to their faces. This lasted his entire life.

In his elementary years, he was so sweet and kind to everyone that his mother tried to teach him to "be firm" and not be so nice when others were trying to hurt or bully him or bring him down. There were times he would feel sorry for the substitute teachers because in middle school other students did not treat them fairly. This made Christian sad, and he would always make an extra effort to be kind to the substitute teachers and say kind things to them after class, reassuring them that they were doing a great job. He would even share his disappointment with his peers when the student teachers were not treated well. He did not like to see other people hurt, in pain, suffering, or being treated poorly and disrespectfully. His compassion and empathy for others were out of this world.

On one occasion, he saw a student hurting and knew it was serious. The student was being bullied, and Christian knew of the student's deep, deep pain. Christian and a staff member discussed the situation and concern for the student. Later, the school staff member wrote us and told us how Christian saved that student's life. It was clear that he had been blessed from an early age with an incredible gift and he carried it with him throughout his life.

When Christian was 15 months old, his sister Kate joined our family and their bond became unbreakable. From a young age, Christian took on the role of the protective older brother, keeping a watchful eye on his sibling. He not only shielded her from harm but also took responsibility for her actions, offering excuses when necessary. Growing up in Christian's radiant light, Kate formed an immeasurable connection with him. Their bond was not only strengthened by their close ages but also by Christian's unwavering commitment to being her guardian. Even as Christian stepped into young adulthood, his sense of protection never wavered. Their closeness was evident when they decided to attend the same college, ensuring that Christian would always be there for Kate when she needed him.

Christian's loving protectiveness continued when our third child, Nicholas, arrived. As Christian laid eyes on Nicholas for the first time, he gently rubbed the little one's head and whispered, "Ah, you're so tiny and cute." Christian always looked out for Nick's well-being, constantly protecting him, and worrying about his safety, especially around our family swimming pool. It became a common occurrence for Christian to excuse himself from elementary school class, feigning illness, just to call home to check on Nick. This level of dedication to his siblings prompted calls from the school, concerned about Christian's frequent visits to the nurse!

In our private moments together, especially following his diagnosis, Christian and I delved into deep conversations about life after death. It was not a typical subject for a father and son, and surely a very delicate one, but I knew it was important to Christian to address the reality of the situation rather than avoiding it. I was reluctant to discuss these matters, preferring to focus on the positive aspects of our lives. However, Christian's wisdom surpassed his years, and he understood the importance of confronting such topics. After our discussions, he expressed his gratitude for being able to have these conversations since it was rare for anyone to broach the subject with him. As a father and husband, I kept these discussions to myself, knowing the pain these discussions would cause to Danielle, Kate, and Nick.

I remember one particular walk we took together, about three months before Christian passed away. In that moment, I was once again blessed with Christian's humor and levity. He said, "You know, Dad, I have one regret in life that I wish I could change." Naturally, I hung onto every word, feeling privileged to be in the presence of someone truly exceptional and wise beyond his years. (This is something that many people who met Christian would say about him.) With effortless charm, he continued, "I wish I had done less homework." I chuckled but then asked if that was truly his only regret. Without hesitation, he replied, "Yes."

Christian had a way of bringing life back into perspective whenever he spoke, and this was just one example of many throughout our journey together. On two occasions during these private moments, Christian emphasized the importance of my presence for the family and reminded me, "You have two other beautiful children to take care of." Once again, he showed his selflessness by thinking of his siblings and their needs. He also told his mother that she, too, would be of great need to Kate and Nick when he was gone. Christian reminded his mother that the disease he had would one day take his life: a fact that she didn't accept but he fully embraced. He told her that her amazing children would need her and that she needed to be strong for them, just like she always was for him. Once again, Christian was well aware of his situation at the tender age of 22 and still took it upon himself to ensure that the people he loved so much—his siblings—would be taken care of when he was no longer here to watch over them.

Christian went to Pine Richland High School and furthered his studies at Robert E. Cook Honors College at Indiana University of Pennsylvania. In the bustling hallways of high school—amid the clamor of teenage ambition and drama—my son navigated his high school years with a rare blend of humor and humility. It was never his aim to stand in the spotlight, yet his natural charisma and understated confidence drew people to him, and it made the drab high school experience a bit brighter for everyone.

Even in his most creatively entertaining moments—such as turning lunchtime into an impromptu comedy club—there remained a gentle undercurrent of humility: He wasn't performing for the applause—he was there to share a smile and lighten the load of academic stress and teenage angst with a laugh. His pranks and playful acts were never mean-spirited, but rather his way of weaving joy into the everyday fabric of school life. Where others saw a cafeteria, he saw a stage: Who else could parade around with a slice of watermelon wedged in his mouth—not as a snack but as a prop in his latest comedy sketch, inducing gales of laughter? This humility shined in what became a memorable event for many.

During his high school senior year, he orchestrated a gathering that could have sparked a confrontation in a setting where egos often clashed—the so-called chess fight—but his involvement delivered camaraderie. In a world where every shuffle and shout could signify conflict, he saw an opportunity for unity and comedy. As onlookers expected a showdown, they instead found themselves surrounding two students deeply immersed in a chess game. The spectacle wasn't about showcasing his cleverness or drawing attention to himself: It was a gentle reminder that at the heart of every expectation lies the opportunity for surprise and unity. The laughter that followed wasn't just for the unexpected twist but for the simplicity of the lesson imparted.

His comfort in his own skin wasn't merely apparent—it was infectious. Elected Prom King not by political maneuvering but by sheer force of likability, he had a way of making every hallway encounter feel like a scene from a feel-good movie. His full head of curly hair, always a half-beat from being tamed, danced as he did: a bit goofy at times, perhaps to catch your eye or (as I suspect) to catch others off guard and send them into a fit of reluctant laughter. He remained the boy who'd rather crack a joke than a textbook (although he was a brilliant student), who saw every person as a friend he hadn't met yet, and who believed that the greatest accolades were the moments shared between people.

In those moments—those brilliantly orchestrated scenes of high school life—my son taught us all a valuable lesson: Life doesn't have to be so serious. With a bit of creativity and a lot of heart, the mundane can become memorable, and every day is an opportunity to make someone smile. In addition to this, he also taught me (perhaps without realizing it) that true strength lies in the ability to bring light to others' lives without needing to stand in the spotlight.

His journey was a testament to the power of humility, a reminder that the most profound impacts often come from the quietest moments. It's evident that high school was not just a chapter in his life, but a canvas on which he painted with broad strokes of joy and subtle hues of humility. He walked the halls not as a figure to be revered, but as a friend to be cherished, leaving behind a legacy that was less about the laughter he elicited and more about the warmth and genuineness he shared.

As I look back on those years, it's clear that high school was more than a stepping stone for him, it was a launching pad. He entered as a boy full of potential and left as a young man who knew the power of laughter, the strength of friendship, and most importantly, the value of being unapologetically himself.

During his brief visit to this Earth, Christian carved a way forward to reach his dreams. In his student years, he studied abroad in Prague (2019) at the Anglo-American University, as well as the Indian Institute of Technology in Calcutta. He completed his Bachelor's degree in International Relations, Asian Studies, and Theater, and graduated magna cum laude from Cook Honors College (Indiana University of Pennsylvania) in 2020.

He gained acting instruction from Randy Kovitz and Alison Rose Saunders (Mosser Casting, Pittsburgh, PA; Pittsburgh CLO Academy; and Keystone Theater, Pittsburgh, PA). His stage, theater, and film credits included *The Company*, *Boeing Boeing*, *The Shape of Things*, *The Music Man*, *Pippin*, *Thoroughly Modern Millie*, *CATS*, and a role as an orphan in *The Dark Knight Rises* (Warner Bros Pictures).

He met the love of his life, Rachael, while studying in Prague. Rachael shared some of their most beautiful moments with us. From the start of their relationship, they complemented each other, and their love was strengthened. Rachael found it amusing when she and Christian started dating, and he was unsure how to handle her silence. She appreciated quiet coexistence and cherished their time together. Initially, Christian filled the silent moments with jokes, stories, or questions, but he grew to appreciate them. He later explained that adjusting to the silence was challenging but it helped him appreciate simplicity: loving-togetherness without the need for words.

Conversely, Rachael told us how Christian had taught her to embrace her outgoing and creative sides. He helped her to learn to laugh at herself instead of being too worried about being embarrassed. He got her to be more social. In this way, they were a good match for each other. She said that sometimes she would joke that they were the "angel" and "devil" on people's shoulders. Unsurprisingly, Christian was the angel.

She told me that the biggest regrets she had were their four-month breakup, along with saying no to his marriage request. She recalled when Christian was getting set up to go start his life in California. At first, they planned to stay together, and he would return after the first year. But she believed that once he went there and people saw him act—and met him in general—he wouldn't be coming home. Indeed, she figured he was going to make it big and everyone was going to adore him. And with that in mind, she got scared and stressed, and didn't know how to handle it. In her own words,

> I tried to keep going, but one day I just woke up so angry. I knew I wasn't over it and I was mad that we didn't fight for each other, and mad at him for suggesting the break. All in all, he just didn't want to make anyone sad, or disappoint anyone, so he did what he thought was best.

Their love survived this turmoil once she contacted him and demanded answers. They both realized then that they loved each other too much to stay apart. Rachael told me that, at that point, she didn't mind him leaving to embrace his acting career. She just wanted to enjoy their time together.

However, the wheel of fate had other plans: It was between the time of this decision and before they met up again in person, that he was diagnosed with cancer. Rachael recalls that it must have been some divine intervention that made her wake up one day knowing that things between them couldn't ever end. She knew that she was meant to be with him until the end—not just because he was sick or because she felt bad—but because that was where she was meant to be.

Apart from the admiration and devotion from us and his girlfriend, the broader network of family and friends observed similar personality traits and deep connections with Christian. His aunt Heather wrote the following about his charismatic personality:

> He was a natural on air. He was also a radio personality and co-host on Local Limelight, a weekly radio show at his college, at the University of Indiana, PA.
>
> At the time of his diagnosis, Christian was planning on heading for Hollywood to pursue a career as an actor, and possibly, a writer. He was always a star. As a family friend recently recalled, "He had such unusual charisma, it's a shame the whole world won't know. But we knew."
>
> The world knew some. At age 14, Christian scored a role in The Dark Knight Rises, a major studio release starring Christian Bale as Batman and Tom Hardy as Bane. Christian packed a lot of expression into his several seconds on screen,

shaking his head of curls with memorable enthusiasm and securing a spot in film history.

A thespian and singer, he also played the lead in many plays at high school. I regret that I didn't see more than only one of his shows. He was a member of the theater group, and performed in the production of various plays.

Did I mention Christian was gorgeous? Perhaps the least important of his many great qualities, but he was a smoke show. His cherubic beauty—big brown eyes, full lips, high cheekbones, symmetrical features, and impossibly thick, glossy, chestnut curls turned heads at three and 23!

Despite his acting roles on stage and in film, Christian remained remarkably humble. Friends often discovered by accident only that he was part of some well-known productions: He never boasted about them. This down-to-earth quality remained with Christian to the end. Most people remember him for this. He could make a person feel special and important, regardless of rank, position, gender, race, age, or culture.

Christian loved his mother's cooking and Italian heritage. I have beautiful photos of their visits all over the world, including to Venice. These photos (like all the other photos with his family) make one thing very clear: his deep love for and devotion to his family. You can see the warmth in his eyes as he gazes at Danielle or his siblings—his gentle smile warming our hearts and his mane of curly locks framing his beautiful face. Danielle and Christian were truly happiest in these moments of sharing their special bond: the one a mother shares with her child. Danielle's Italian heritage and nurturing warmth are evident in her journal entry about the *pizzelle* cookie offered to her young son:

> I offer you an Italian pizzelle cookie and you reach for it and hold it gently in your hand. You pause, holding the cookie between your little pointer finger and your thumb. You admire its beauty, intricate shape, delicateness, and unique details. Most children of your age would begin eating it straight away, ignoring all the beauty that the cookie holds. Not you. You seek out the beauty and appreciate it. You meditate on the cookie

without even knowing what meditation is at the tender age of three. You see the cookie for what it is, you stay focused on it and its details. And then you notice that the pizzelle is like something else, full of beauty that you have experienced before. You look at me and say with a big smile and joyful voice, "Look Mommy, it's just like the stained glass window in our church" (Sacred Heart Church, Shadyside). Only then do you begin to take small, appreciative, slow bites as you savor every crumb.

The origin of the *pizzelle* cookie is noteworthy here. It is believed to be the oldest known cookie in the world and originated from the Abruzzo region in the south-central part of Italy. It's said to have developed from the Roman *crustulum* (an ancient cookie recipe). To this day, two feuding villages (Salle and Colcullo) still argue the rights to the claim of its origin.

The origin goes back to the feast day of San Domenico, also known as the Festival of the Snakes. Legend tells us the history of a village overrun by snakes, in which the Benedictine monk (San Domenico) cleared out the serpents after being summoned. The village celebrated this with the famous cookie. The festival still takes place in Italy every year on the 1st of May.

*Pizzelles*, resembling waffle cookies, are traditionally made with eggs, flour, sugar, and oil or butter. They are often anise-flavored, but variations include vanilla or lemon zest. The intricate designs on *pizzelle* can feature noble family crests or snowflake patterns. These patterns are imprinted using a heated, long-handled iron. The dough, stamped on both sides, can be molded into various shapes, reminiscent of the famous tubular *cannoli*. It is filled with creamy fillings and turns crispy upon cooling.

The delicacy is famously offered during Christmas and Easter and is abundantly present at wedding ceremonies. As with most Italian food, seasonal and celebratory relevance goes together with the time of serving specific culinary delights. The cookie's significance during the most important Christian annual celebrations remains prominent here: Interestingly, Christian made an instant connection with its spiritual relevance by comparing the patterned design on the *pizzelle* with our church window designs.

## Faced With the Unthinkable

Christian always took an optimistic view of life. Even after his diagnosis, he faced his challenges with understanding and acceptance. He committed himself to maintaining his kindhearted and compassionate nature and he showed his love to all who crossed his path.

The women in Christian's life felt deeply loved. He cherished their presence and made it visible by showing his love with small but meaningful gestures. His intuitiveness and eye for detail became evident through some of their journal entries. Although it's still challenging for his sister, Kate, to publicly share her experiences with Christian, I am happy to share the impressions from his mother, Danielle, and his girlfriend, Rachael with you.

### *A Mother's Journal*

Christian always had so much love and was always aware of other people's suffering. He wanted to make sure that people felt loved and happy.

> Christian is almost eight years young. (2004)
>
> Last week, Christian watched Cheaper by the Dozen with the entire family. The end of the movie made him sad and he began to cry. He told each of us individually how he loved us and gave everyone a big hug and said, "Family means love and hope." He is so precious.
>
> Today, Grandma and Grandpa Wysocki came to our house to visit. Christian kept putting his arm around Grandma, hugging her, and sitting close to her. She has dementia and it's getting

worse. She doesn't recognize family members and keeps saying, "What a beautiful little girl" to Christian with all his locks of curls and full long head of hair. He never corrects her and allows her to refer to him incorrectly. He's aware that she does not mean it and has something causing the comments.

She really loves his hugs and attention. Today, it made Grandpa so happy to observe this love.

Christian never had a to-do list: it was always a *to-love list*. That is how he navigated life. After chemo started, we had some memorable and very emotional exchanges. I will never forget the day his curls fell to the earth... Around the time when chemo started, Christian woke up one day and said, "Mom and Dad, I'm going to shave my head today." His hair was starting to fall out due to the chemotherapy drug Abraxane. Christian knew his hair loss was imminent and he wanted to manage his situation by shaving it all off at once instead of experiencing it fall out piece by piece, section by section.

As the "keeper" of his beautiful mane of curls for his lifetime, and as his mother, you can only imagine my brief frenzy. I was hoping that the particular chemotherapy treatment he was getting wouldn't take away all his curls. I was hoping it would just cure him quickly and there would be no need. At this point, none of his hair had dramatically fallen out and I was determined that our sweet, loving Christian would survive his cancer and keep his beautiful full head of hair. I held on to the thought that after the shaving of his trademark long, soft, curly, brown locks they would return to a full head of hair on my beautiful son's head one day soon.

Up to that time, Christian had been on Zoom calls with the full-time job he took at Automatic Data Processing (ADP), a human resources software company. He showed up every day for work on the computer screen—with a full head of curly hair, bouncing with every movement and gesture he made. After Christian's announcement of shaving his head, in the brisk morning, we went into the frosted backyard. Christian sat on his great-great-grandmother's chair (Anna Marcinko) and his father began to shave his full head of curls. It didn't bother Christian. He was ready to do this. As he saw his image in his cell phone's reflection, he laughed and said he looked like Skrillex, a popular American DJ and music producer! He said that his head felt colder, but that he liked the way he looked.

When his shaved head was done, he smiled proudly, embracing his new look. I gathered some curls from the ground. For a moment I thought I should keep them all, but then my mind automatically said, "Not to worry, they will grow back again." So, I knelt on the stone patio, and with Christian's help, I gathered only a few darker curls as they lay in a gentle pile. I had so much hope for Christian to be healed: Of course, his full, fabulous, signature curls would grow back soon, once that awful period of our lives was "fixed."

Christian remained positive and comforted me even during this life-changing moment. He was always so positive, smart, and wise beyond his years. There was nothing sad about this moment for Christian—he was excited to embrace his "new look." I wanted to ease the change by saying, "It looks terrific." Christian, sensing my hidden anguish, responded, "It's just hair, it will grow back, and what's most important is what is inside your head, not on top of it." I grew to love the way his short hair made his eyes sparkle and shine—just like his heart and personality!

When he showed up for work, logging into his morning Zoom call with his ADP team—shaved head and all—his teammates who viewed him first were shocked. "Where did your full head of curls go?" they asked. Christian explained that he "just felt like trying something new." He did not want his colleagues to know that he had cancer. He did not want to burden them. He did not want them to feel bad or sad. He just wanted to be his normal self: always gifting joy.

> I ask myself repeatedly, "How did this happen?" How is it possible that a few months before his diagnosis, our family unit of five spent a week traveling out west, exploring, sharing stories, cooking together, hiking in nature, and loving each other deeply at the Grand Canyon? This was the Christmas of quiet and us enjoying the gifts of our family being together in nature: doing the simple things, creating memories. These were our gifts to one another. Christian and Nick just started to get to know each other since Nick was now 16. I'm in shock about this tornado spinning out of control through my family. I need

to stay sharp and focused. We need to figure it all out because we have to save our son.

For a whole year, we searched for a cure. My husband never stopped calling top doctors all over the country. We communicated with the Cholangiocarcinoma Foundation and the best medical personnel in the world. Our family and extended family members stood together in a supportive network to help my sweet Christian. It was like being on a bullet train—we knew we were pressed for time.

Christian trusted us to navigate this process, and we did our best. The only time when he voiced his opinion about his entrusted care was a few months before his passing. After the T-cell trial, and the genetic mutation attempt, he sat with me on the sofa and calmly said, "Mom, I want you to know that if this next trial doesn't work, then I'm okay with things and I don't desire to try more." He was physically exhausted at the time as he confronted the trajectory of his illness and its outcome. I think he preferred to spend quality time with his family after that. He had made his peace.

> Christian and I have been up for hours. He is in physical pain, I'm in emotional pain. He's finally resting somewhat peacefully with Maple [his dog] under his left arm. I gave him the rosary beads to hold in his right hand and told him that it's like holding the Blessed Mother Mary's hand. Just before he fell asleep, Christian told me that he made his peace and he wants to be with Christ.
>
> As he said that, I looked out the window at the break of dawn and saw a strong and radiant buck on the hillside in the morning glow. Then a tiny spotted fawn appeared and playfully ran along the hillside. The frolicking fawn looked around and then ran off after the buck.
>
> Was the buck my father, who had recently passed? Was the fawn my darling Christian, excited to follow him to heaven?

The last time Christian slept overnight in the hospital was in July 2021. I slept next to him, pushing the lounge chair up to his bed so we could be close enough to hold hands. The next day, the nurses and doctors were making their rounds and we planned to bring him home. There was much going on, and Christian noticed me having difficulty with the situation. (I was emotional because of discussions I had had with his doctor in the hallway.) Christian came up to me, hugged me, and said, "Mom, treat your emotions like visitors. They are just passing through."

He said this so eloquently and peacefully. I asked him to repeat those words to me. Once again, there he was, calming me with his wisdom: My sweet Christian comforting me with his gift of kind words. In his profound wisdom, he gave me the tools to use and remember whenever overwhelming emotions appear. He taught me that emotions come and go and that I shouldn't hold on to them for too long. And he knew that I would need to be reminded of these words when he was gone.

Christian never complained. He knew there was no purpose in that. So, he didn't. The only time I recall him voicing a complaint was when his girlfriend, Rachael, visited us and I made breakfast for everyone. He had trouble swallowing the French toast and he said in his sweetest voice: "I can't even eat my mother's good home cooking anymore." I'm sure those words went past everybody in that room, but I never forgot them. I always took such love and joy in cooking for my family. It was one of the greatest joys of my life to nourish Christian. He always enjoyed what I prepared, told me how much he enjoyed it, and thanked me for preparing it for him. He would even eat my burnt toast and say, "Thank you, it was delicious!" So, to hear him say these words broke my heart even more.

I knew the days of nurturing him with his favorite food were slowly dissipating as the tumor grew and blocked his ability to digest food. When we reached the point where he was on the verge of taking only liquids, I knew that he would never eat another of my Italian ricotta cheese cookies for Christmas or Easter again. Nor would he eat my pasta bolognese, beef carnitas or Italian wedding soup. No pork and sauerkraut on New Year's Day. He wouldn't even eat my Chambord birthday cake, or any of the many things I had prepared so lovingly for my family throughout his life. I held on to his appreciation for that, but that in itself was a painful loss.

Christian never expressed his anger or frustration at the illness that was taking his life away from him, even during the most challenging periods. Rather, he would calmly embrace me and comfort me when I cursed his cancer by saying, "Mom, I would never use those words or refer to my cancer in that manner. I consider it an honorable adversary of mine and respect it." I had even made a note of this in my journal:

> Too much love in your heart and soul to hate.
>
> My sweet child, your love is endless, it permeates space and continues to shine.
>
> How is it that with all your beauty, grace, brilliance, and love you could not even speak ill or hate the disease inside of you even though it was slowly taking you away from your family: the people and the life you loved so much.
>
> Instead, you told me it was an "honorable adversary."
>
> I was sorry for saying such foul words in a moment of fear and frustration. I despised it the moment that it made its awful appearance in our lives.
>
> You taught me humility, gratitude, strength, and grace—you are not of this world, my darling Christian.

His greatest pain was to see his friends and family—the people he loved and cared for so much—feel sad or suffer because of his illness. In loving ways, he apologized to me for having his illness. He saw his purpose in life as bringing unconditional joy, hope, love, laughter, and kindness to everyone. Throughout his illness, he remained lighthearted and saw the humor in every circumstance while finding pockets of joy in everyday events.

Even when he needed surgery for the pain in his back, he would make the most of it and look for something good. (Like the time when he said the chemo running through his veins had platinum in it and that it was more valuable than gold.) He was a true follower of anything retro and '80s, and he recalled with so much joy that the surgeons who operated on his spine were listening to '80s music while they operated.

He was so happy to have such a wonderful team of doctors who came from all walks of life: female, male, Jewish, Muslim, Indian, and American. He loved the diversity of his team.

Before passing the narrative back over to Chris, I'd like to share a few sweet stories from Christian's childhood days that characterize his youthful ways, courtesy of my journal:

> When he was three, we once flew from Pittsburgh to Miami. We left a cold, snowy Pittsburgh in February to find some warmth in Miami. From the airport we went to have some lunch on the water and Christian was aware of the warmth and beauty of our new surroundings. He was standing on my lap and the warm ocean breeze was blowing as he leaned into the wind with the biggest smile on his face and said, "Mommy, kiss the wind!" I'll never forget that. I wrote that down in my journal. He kept leaning into the warm wind and said kiss the wind. Until this day, whenever the breeze touches my face, I am taken back to those special moments and I feel how he is kissing me gently on my forehead and cheeks as he used to do so often.
>
> On another occasion, he watched me and his father hugging and laughing and said to his aunt and uncle, "They're so much in love."
>
> Christian loved traveling. He enjoyed the journey in a mindful way, not only rushing toward the destination, but taking in all the details en route to his destination. He enjoyed every aspect of the traveling and would embark on a new discovery, often going off the beaten track to find something new—never hurrying. It was on these trips that he cherished new connections with people from all over the world, and he took the time to appreciate what the trip had to offer, whether it was scenery, a cultural encounter, or new discoveries about life.
>
> He loved airports. Airports' hustle and bustle of people moving around and exploring the world excited him. When he saw a plane in the sky, he would stop and look at it with such curiosity. The smallest things delighted him and stirred his

imagination. He would often say, "I wonder where that plane is headed. I wonder who the people are, and what their plans are for their travels." We had incredible vacations with our children. Some spent at home and others traveling all over the world. Once, when we returned from Disneyworld—Christian was still very young—we asked him what the best part of his vacation was, and he excitedly replied, "The airport!"

Christian loved all living things, especially the sea and its creatures. But he also loved the Earth's animals, trees, and plants. His favorite tree was the ginkgo tree—perhaps because the tree originated in East Asia and he loved Asian studies. He especially loved the golden yellow color of the changing trees in fall. The things he loved as a child are a sure indication of his free-spirited character: He loved kites, he was fascinated by travel, and the sea—and sailing on it—made him quite happy. Every spring, a mother bunny would appear in our yard, and Christian and I would call her Angel. We marveled at her hopping through the yard in the early morning and late evening hours. I always told him that he was blessed with a beautiful outside appearance, accompanied by a beautiful heart, mind, and soul. He used these gifts for the good of others and bestowed them lovingly on all whom he encountered. In turn, even though not intentionally sought, this enhanced his feelings of gratitude, love, and happiness.

Christian lived with so much beauty and grace. He was always the wisest person in the room. Despite the imminent loss of everything he loved—including his family, friends, and future dreams—he managed to keep it together. We were losing him, and *we* could hardly keep it together. He never showed his suffering, though—so that we wouldn't suffer more.

It was truly a privilege to watch Christian's life unfold. It was the most remarkable and joyful thing to be a part of his earthly journey. I am deeply blessed to have been his mother: truly, a lifetime honor and privilege. He loved me unconditionally, and that is very rare to find.

# *Rachael's Journal*

Rachael told us that she always thought Christian would recover completely up until the last week of his illness. So, the diagnosis never truly hit her until then. He remained the most loving, caring, and thoughtful person despite his suffering. It never dimmed his humor and he still made light out of even the darkest moments. Nothing stopped him from being who he was. Rachael said it was tough to talk about the last days of his life with us all. But she kept a journal during that harrowing last month. She continues to read those entries to this day to fill her heart with the joy she and Christian had shared, even during their more challenging days. It's heartbreaking for me to read her notes and rewrite them, so I'll honor their beautiful bond by sharing her exact words and memories:

> I remember him saying once, "I am sorry I won't be able to protect you and keep you safe." He was getting weaker, but I told him it was okay, because it was my turn to protect him.
>
> We went to a little Airbnb cottage one weekend near Lancaster. It was so wonderful: It even started snowing and it was like nothing was wrong with the world. I remember us just enjoying each other's company, not even having to talk.
>
> I remember the last summer. It was right after Christian's grandfather died. I was able to come up and surprise him as I drove straight from work. Christian teared up and gave me a bear hug. Honestly, I think I was the one who needed to see him more: He was my rock, you know?
>
> I remember when he had to shave his hair. He was sad because it was such a huge part of his identity, but he still managed to keep his head up. He also rocked the bald look, and somehow stayed just as handsome, if not more handsome! I think because it made his eyes more prominent.
>
> Once, during the last few weeks when Christian was in a deep sleep, I fell, and he woke up with his eyes wide open and immediately said he needed to get up and help me. Then, when

I sat next to him, he held my hand tight against his chest and fell back asleep like that.

I miss his doodles and drawings. He would always make me stickers out of the postal stickers.

I look at your face and behind it is just a sea of stars.

I tell you that you look beautiful and you respond with, "You look beautiful." I tell you that I love you and you respond with, "I love you more."

Some random entries:

He called me his dream girl.

His favorite kids movie is Ratatouille.

He has more freckles on his nose and on his right eyebrow—that's beautiful.

He desperately wanted a diet Sprite!

He still has me on his phone listed as "cricket provider."

Christian said he wanted to marry me "up there," which I think meant in heaven.

He suggested having copious birds in the trees at our wedding, humorously noting that it might lead to a messy surprise for the cars below, much to the guests' amusement.

His eyes are more yellow today, but the irises are still a beautiful brown.

Christian's dad told him that he wanted to "be like him when he grew up" and Christian said, "Don't do that, you'll be dead by 30."

Even though he was so sick, he surprised me with a silver and malachite ring. He knew it was my favorite stone, and he had his dad help him purchase it. He picked it out. It came in a little white box and it was so beautiful.

At midnight, he was up for the bathroom. When we went back to bed and said our goodnights, he said, "My love for you will never die."

While half-asleep on Dilaudid [a very strong opioid pain reliever often used to treat cancer patients, which has severe side-effects] he said, "I really don't want to make international news right now. I hope I don't sound too fond of myself because I don't like to flaunt."

Last night, he was in a lot of pain when the Dilaudid wore off. He is now on a constant drip. We had a conversation about death and heaven with his dad.

He asked us, "Am I a good person? Did I do right by God? I want to make sure I do right by God."

Every time I say his name he opens his eyes.

When I go to the shower, he asks me where I am.

A couple of nights ago [August, 2021], we thought it was his time, and we gathered around him. We cried. We lit candles, shared stories, and assured him of our love. At some point in the morning, he woke up and said it was creepy that we were all staring at him and crying. He said, "What do you think, I'm dying or something?"

I had to fly home for school and said goodbye to Christian. I asked him if he would marry me when he got better. He said he'd love too. Our last words were I love you. I hope this wasn't our last goodbye.

He sent me two videos since I have been home. They are so sweet and loving, but he looks so weak: It's heartbreaking.

He passed at 12:38 p.m. on the first of September, 2021, exactly three years from the day we met in Prague. He wore my

Providence sweatshirt to the crematorium. I wanted to hold him to the end. He loved that sweatshirt and had been wearing it for a week. I also put the socks I made him for Christmas on his feet: the custom-made ones with pictures of Maple and Lula [his dogs] on them, so they could protect him until the end too.

His last words to me were, "I love you."

Then he died with me caressing his face and kissing his forehead.

His spirit is not gone.

I promised him I would meet him up there, whatever that is.

When I told Uncle David about Christian's last words, my nose immediately started bleeding. (The second, third, and fourth times me and Christian kissed, I got a nose bleed on him. He would always laugh and tease me with his cute smile.)

Christian was deeply loved by all of us and this is evident in both his mother's and girlfriend's journal entries. The most beautiful thing about him was that he returned our love so generously, respectfully, and unconditionally. It takes a special person to receive love. A gentle soul is needed to reciprocate such love even more.

## Concluding Thoughts: Inspired by Christian

Christian's radiant spirit is a guiding light for us during challenging times. He has been the guiding light in writing this book. Let's honor his example by remembering his ways, as follows:

- Live with acceptance. Strive for optimism. Remain humble, even in the face of despair.

- Check in on others. Nurture human connection. Stay devoted to living mindfully, daily. Find pockets of joy in everyday events and in the mundane. Intentionally make someone feel special, unconditionally.

- Strive for empathy. Honor connection and show your love. Open your heart to receive love.

- Confront your fears and challenges. Embrace your emotions as they are passing through you. Don't deny them their rightful place in your journey.

- Most of all—never take life too seriously. Remember to "kiss the wind."

# Chapter 2:

# The Change

*Be grateful for whoever comes, because each has been sent as a guide from beyond.* – Rumi

On August 26th, 2020, Christian was diagnosed with a rare terminal cancer: cholangiocarcinoma. Despite learning about his fatal diagnosis, Christian remained remarkably positive throughout his challenging journey. He would routinely ask all of those around him *"What's good about today?"* It was his continual method of encouraging all of us to see the good in each day and grasp the opportunities that come our way. His sense of gratitude and humility was very rare. Indeed, it became one of the many profound legacies he left us.

We have used his mantra to name his website and we continue to share it with the world. Perhaps his words were an echo to himself after the realization that he was faced with such a difficult journey. Still, he carried this burden with grace, his tale of hope illuminating the paths of many.

## The Question That Changed Everything

Danielle wrote in her journal that Christian had boundless energy and curiosity from a young age, which he carried with him throughout his life. He was an avid reader with a photographic memory. When he became ill, as much as this circumstance was undesirable, it presented him with a new subject upon which he could devote his curiosity. He wanted to understand everything about his illness and was always engaged with his doctors. But his curiosity surpassed the borders of his own life. Indeed, he wanted to learn more about *their* lives: What brought them to study and treat this cancer? Christian maintained his focus on his specialist care team instead of on himself. He was grateful for the diversity of his medical team and appreciated all they did for him. One of his biggest desires was to offer his body for medical research to find a life-changing cure.

On a fateful day in August 2020, Christian and I found ourselves at Hillman Cancer Institute in Pittsburgh, PA. Christian's journey began with a routine blood test, instigated by his back pain and ailing health. To ensure his health was in order, we followed up with a CT scan. Little did we know that his visit would change our lives forever. Deep down, I tried to reassure my son that this was likely just a precautionary measure, something all medical institutions do. But when I made that phone call, the words I heard sent a chill down my spine—they had found a "scar" on his liver.

Before we embarked on our journey to Hillman Cancer Institute, I turned to the internet for answers. I anguishly searched for information about scars on the liver, desperately hoping to find that it might not be a big deal. Perhaps this scar had been there all along, benignly residing within him. The COVID-19 pandemic was at its peak at this time, and so only one family member was allowed to accompany Christian. I assured Danielle that I would take him and we would be back in no time to continue our beautiful life, after this brief though notably stressful interruption.

As we made our way to the institute, I repeated words of comfort to my calm son, assuring him that there was nothing to worry about. It was likely just a bruise, I told him, and the explanation for his off-blood count was simply that this little scar was causing some chaos in his body. Taking antibiotics would be the easy fix, or so I believed.

Upon arrival, we were escorted into a small room, masks concealing our faces. Despite the circumstances, I clung to the hope that Christian was healthy and invincible. But when the doors swung open, revealing five doctors in white lab coats, my heart sank. Their eyes spoke volumes and I knew instantly that my beautiful son was in trouble. I didn't need to see their faces; their eyes betrayed the gravity of the news they were about to deliver. A sickening feeling washed over me, and darkness crept into my vision.

Christian, on the other hand, greeted everyone with a radiant smile filled with love, joy, and humor. He exuded an unwavering positivity, devoid of any doubt or concern. Even in that room, he cracked jokes to lighten the mood and put the doctors at ease. The lead liver doctor instructed Christian to remove his shirt and lean back, and that's when I noticed a large, round bump on his lower abdomen. As Christian put his shirt back on, the doctor uttered the words that shattered our world: "Christian, you have cancer. You have a grapefruit-sized tumor on your liver."

I stood beside my son, my hands trembling as those words hung in the air. My legs felt weak, and my eyes grew heavy—the weight of the world was crashing down on me. But in that moment, Christian displayed a superpower. He sensed my pain and fear. He immediately reached out to hold me, locking eyes with me as if we were the only two people in that room. "Dad, don't worry," he reassured me with his unwavering voice of strength. "I am fine, I will be okay." As he helped me sit still, Christian turned his attention back to the doctor and asked the question that took everyone by surprise: "How much time do I have left?" It was as if he had a premonition of what was to come.

The doctor hesitated, not wanting to answer, but Christian knew the truth. Time was not on his side. Yet, amid this devastating news, I never saw Christian get upset or question why this was happening. On the contrary, he expressed gratitude to everyone in that room, thanking them for their presence and wishing them a wonderful day. In that room, I bore witness to something truly remarkable. Christian, despite being handed a death sentence, possessed an unbreakable spirit that defied all odds. Amid unimaginable pain and suffering, he exuded an aura of joy and beauty that captivated those around him. It was as if he possessed a unique perspective on the world, perceiving its wonders in a way that eluded the rest of us. While we focus on the minutiae of everyday life (although in this particular moment, my focus was on the unfolding tragedy), Christian saw beyond the surface, embracing the grandeur of existence. For Christian, beauty manifested itself in the form of the doctors who attended to him, that day and always. Their presence was a testament to the remarkable qualities that Christian possessed. It wasn't a solitary occurrence but a recurring theme that unfolded each time he crossed paths with another individual. Every interaction became an opportunity for Christian to display his extraordinary behavior, leaving a lasting impact on all who encountered him.

During Christian's treatment, we ventured to renowned medical centers such as Sloan Kettering, Johns Hopkins, Cleveland Clinic, and Massachusetts General. Unexpectedly, a nurse from one of these facilities reached out to me, bending the rules of protocol and confidentiality. She expressed her need to share a personal experience, one that had transformed her life. As a wheelchair attendant, she had the privilege of transporting Christian within the hospital. Along their journey, it was customary to point out art installations and public displays, in the hope of offering some solace to the patients. However, this encounter with Christian proved to be far from ordinary.

The nurse explained that during their hour-long conversation, Christian focused solely on her. He sought to ensure her comfort and happiness, inquiring about her life and sharing lighthearted moments that brought laughter to her heart. Gratitude emanated from Christian as he expressed his appreciation for getting to know her and learning about her experiences. His sole desire was to convey her importance, leaving her day brimming with joy. Overwhelmed with emotion, the nurse confided in me, tears streaming down her cheeks, "He owed me nothing, yet he gave me everything." In the depths of his dire circumstances, Christian's concern was solely for her well-being.

This account is just one of many that exemplify Christian's extraordinary nature, both prior to and following his diagnosis. Time and again, he defied expectations and touched the lives of those around him, leaving an indelible mark on their lives.

I've embarked on an urgent quest to capture the very essence of Christian's remarkable presence. How does one master the art of transforming each day into a captivating and joyous adventure amid the constant barrage of challenges, disappointments, suffering, despair, and the sheer difficulties of daily life? Our language falls short, but there's one word that keeps resurfacing: gratitude.

Recently, I stumbled upon a profound quote that halted me in my tracks: "Dead people receive more flowers than the living ones because regret is stronger than gratitude" (Goodreads, n.d.). Just let that sink in for a moment. It hit me like a tidal wave. Contemplating this triggered several thoughts. One reason regret holds such power is that we find ourselves trapped in the past more often than not. Instead of embracing the present, we spend each day dwelling on the one that came before it. We replay scenarios, wondering what we could or should have done differently, and we endlessly ruminate on how others have wronged us. In this cycle, we become so consumed by the past that we completely miss out on the wonders unfolding before us in the here and now.

Similarly, by fixating on the future, we also inadvertently skip over the present moment, only to later regret our oversight. Little do we realize that the true power, joy, rewards, connections, and love lie within the present. It is the only reality, for our fears of the future and regrets of the past are nothing but diluted perceptions. Happiness and gratitude reside in embracing the present moment, in being fully present.

Christian was always fully present—every moment, and every day.

## The Art of Pausing

That moment when something triggers our thoughts and makes them change direction—I call that the art of pausing. For a moment in time, we halt and think again, redirect, reframe, rewrite, or rechallenge our paths.

As a father witnessing my son's valiant battle with cancer at the tender age of 22, I was introduced to his transformative power in its most poignant form. Christian, with his unwavering spirit, taught us that within the pauses, life reveals its most profound beauties and truths. Amid treatments and trials, Christian found solace in the stillness. It was in these quiet moments that he uncovered the essence of living—not in the grand events, but in the simple joys that each day brings: a sunrise that paints the sky with hope, the laughter shared in fleeting moments, the quietude that follows a storm—all revealing a world washed anew. These were the snapshots of beauty he cherished. To him, pausing was not a cessation but an embrace of life's depths, a way to drink in the beauty that might otherwise be lost in life's relentless pace.

Christian's pauses were filled with reflection and revelation. They allowed him to meet life with grace, to see beyond his pain, and to find gratitude in the present. This act of pausing became a gift he bestowed upon us, a legacy that continues to unfold. Through his eyes, we learned that to pause is to allow ourselves the space to breathe, to feel deeply, and to connect with the essence of our being. It's in these pauses that we find resilience, draw strength, and rekindle our joy for life. The "power of the pause" in Christian's journey was a testament to his extraordinary character.

It reminded us that even in the shadow of adversity, there is beauty to be found, lessons to be learned, and love to be shared. His brief life was a profound narrative of how pausing in appreciation of daily life can transform our understanding of life itself. As I continue on this path, the echoes of Christian's legacy guide me. The art of pausing has become a compass, directing me to find beauty in the ordinary, strength in stillness, and wisdom in silence. It is a reminder that in life's chaos, there is always an opportunity to find peace, to celebrate life, and to embrace the moment with all its wonders.

## *Cholangiocarcinoma: Bile Duct Cancer*

Hospitals are like vacuumed spaces where the focus shifts to one-dimensional healing. Walking down the corridors of various wards with bandaged people, moaning voices, crying babies, and the ever-present scent of antibacterial substances is enough to send one down a time-travel journey that stirs up copious emotions. When one adds the element of a life-and-death scenario, all of these things intensify.

It made no sense that Christian would get this cancer, considering the rarity of the illness and its related statistical data. I would often ask, "Why? Why *Christian?*" Our daughter, Kate, once said to her mother, "Why *not* Christian? Mom, if you wanted to change many, many lives for the better, then why wouldn't you take Christian?" She was right, and in her youthful way, she gently guided our thoughts. Christian had such an impact on his peers, friends, teachers, family, work associates, and strangers. How could he not be a guiding light for the world's brokenness?

There are three types of cholangiocarcinoma—better known as bile duct cancer. These are classified according to their location in the liver. Intrahepatic (within the small bile ducts), perihilar (where the ducts join and leave the liver), and extrahepatic (outside the liver area) cholangiocarcinoma. Accounting for less than 10% of the cancer, the intrahepatic type is the least common of the bile duct cancers.

The malignant tumors are normally so deep and small that they're difficult to find during a physical exam. They're like slumbering enemies in the body, generally only diagnosed at an advanced stage. Once they penetrate the bile duct wall, though, they easily and quickly infect other nearby organs, growing aggressively all the while. Because of their quiet and slow growth in the beginning stages, they are initially not easily detected. In fact, there are no observable symptoms at that point. This quiet infestation and undetectable nature make them one of the most challenging cancers to treat.

This rare and aggressive cancer is similar to pancreatic cancer, but less common and more fatal. The bile ducts are the small tubes that transport bile (the liver fluid assisting digestion) from the liver to the gallbladder or the small intestines. The gallbladder stores the bile, while the small intestines use bile to break down food fats.

The cancer starts by spreading to blood vessels and then to the adjacent organs and tissues such as the liver, stomach, intestines, diaphragm, and lymph nodes. Eventually, it enters the abdominal lining and bones—but mostly the lungs at a later stage when it becomes almost impossible to cure. The cancer is grouped into five stages by medical doctors, based on the size and spread of the cancer. These are as follows:

1. Stages one to three may show no symptoms unless a bile duct has been blocked by the tumor.

2. After stage three, symptoms appear such as jaundice, itchy skin, dark-colored urine, or chalky and pale stools. The patient may also experience stomach pain and vomiting.

3. As it progresses to specific parts of the body, related areas may also get infused with pain and symptoms.

Doctors may furthermore diagnose the cancer in terms of resectable, unresectable but localized, or metastatic phases. Bile duct surgery is the primary treatment option in the early stages of the cancer. Surgical removal offers the only prospect (albeit a minutely small percentage) for a cure. However, only a small percentage can be surgically treated during the resectable stage. In the metastatic phase, the cancer has spread and reached a phase of infestation that cannot be stopped.

Treatment procedures mostly include targeted therapy, immunotherapy, radiation, and chemotherapy, or sometimes a combination of these options. There are also some emerging treatments under investigation, and scientific progress shows a keen interest in chimeric antigen receptor T-cell (CAR T-cell) therapy treatment. This aims at helping the patient's immune system and its T-cells fight cancer by recognizing and killing foreign cells in the body. This procedure is primarily used for blood cancers (such as leukemia and lymphoma) but ongoing research targets its efficiency for other cancer treatments and it looks promising. Christian waited for many months to be considered for a T-cell procedure. According to Healthline (Hersh & Barlow, 2022, para 4), the process is as follows:

> T-cells are cells in your immune system. They bind to proteins on the surface of cells your body doesn't recognize, also called foreign cells. Some T-cells destroy these cells themselves, while other types signal the rest of your immune system to destroy those foreign cells.
>
> Each type of T-cell only bonds to one type of protein. So, to have your immune system fight cancer cells, you need T-cells with certain receptors. These receptors allow them to bind to the specific cancer cell protein. The process of making these cells to fight cancer is called CAR-T therapy.

The prognosis is expressed in three stages and the survival rate remains at less than 25%. Of course, statistics are based on facts but with time, these ratios change and we should always remember that scientists are constantly making breakthroughs and creating new sources of hope for people with terminal illnesses. The fatality rate of cancer has certainly declined over the past few decades.

Toward the final stages of this cancer, the focus shifts to treatment options that improve quality of life and life expectancy. To enhance overall wellness at this advanced stage of bile duct cancer, the focus shifts mainly to palliative care and symptoms or discomfort relief treatment that reduces pain and nausea. Less than 10,000 bile duct cancer patients are diagnosed annually in the US and most of these patients are older than 65 years. This makes Christian's diagnosis even more shocking.

This is by no means a detailed account of this rare cancer's trajectory and symptoms. I am merely trying to summarize the disease in an understandable way. I would suggest consulting a professional immediately if you suspect similar signs. The Johns Hopkins website (www.hopkinsmedicine.org) is also highly informative.

## The Bright Side: Harnessing Positive Power

Christian had a unique perspective on positivity and gratitude, and it showed in his resilience. He had the ability to see the good in challenging situations and remain joyful despite hardship. This character trait was a huge inspiration to us. His friends, medical personnel, and even strangers paid tribute to his unique ability to turn every moment into something memorable.

Danielle wrote in her journal how Christian was always pleasant, happy, content, loving, kind, and whimsical too. They would go grocery shopping together and if a song was playing that they liked, they would dance and sing down the aisles while shopping. He would walk beside her holding her hand, or with his arms around her. He loved his family so much. He was truly grateful for all we did for him, before he got sick and after... We were so close: our five-member team. Christian was the kind of person who would do anything for you and never expect anything in return. With Christian, we never stopped dancing and singing together. Even with family gatherings and festive celebrations, we would find the opportunity to sing and dance together, much to the amusement of all.

## *CaringBridge Journal Entries*

The globally used *CaringBridge* website provides a communication platform for patients and families facing various medical conditions, such as terminal illnesses. It connects a community by creating a valuable network of support, providing support to the loved ones and connecting them to caregivers during their healing journey. It also prioritizes the patient's privacy, provides an ad-free communication platform, and offers valuable and hassle-free group updates to the patient's friends and family. Ultimately, their vision is to help people feel less alone when facing adverse health conditions.

Our family decided to open such a platform for communication in support of Christian's cancer journey. We had tremendous feedback of love, support, faith, hope, and nurturing provisions that helped us through this time. In a way, it also helped us face the reality of the long journey between hope and acceptance, and it deepened our faith in the presence of a higher being.

Danielle and I undertook the daunting task of writing down reflections and actions on this formidable new journey that we were facing. Needless to say, the journal is laced with emotions, but also with positivity—as this was a crucial element of Christian's journey. He kept us inspired and grateful along the way, despite the challenges and the pain. I'll share some highlights of the *CaringBridge* reflections here. You can find more on the site: www.caringbridge.org/visit/christiancochran. Little did we know that one year later, our world would face inconceivable change.

*September 9, 2020*

First Chemo Day: Starting this journey today. Christian started chemotherapy for his cancer at 8 am this morning. Christian's spirits are high because we're going to beat this thing.

*September 21, 2020*

Christian had a very good weekend. We sat outside by the fire pit two nights in a row, telling stories and filling our little part of the world with laughter. Christian always finds a way to make us laugh so much.

During September, we had both good and challenging days. The blood work test results indicated that Christian's body was responding well to the treatment. That was welcome news as it guided our aim of keeping him as healthy as possible while we learned and fought our way through new trials. Not only was Christian a unique soul, but so was this cancer, as it had turned out. Nonetheless, he remained positive with his uplifting approach. He sincerely wanted to help others, and through his ordeal, he aimed to be at the forefront of this.

We called ourselves the "CC Advisory Group." It was made up of myself, Danielle, Christian, my brother-in-law, David, and my sister-in-law, Bridget. This CC Advisory Group had many video calls with doctors from Pittsburgh Hillman and Sloan Kettering Cancer Center, NYC. In between these, our family remained adamant about maintaining a routine with visits from Kate from college and keeping Christian and Kate's podcast show going strong. These events usually lifted our spirits and blessed our moments with normal activities and laughter—true sunshine moments during turbulent times. You can follow their show at this link: bit.ly/4bkAr4J

I remember waking up one morning to find this incredible message positioned boldly in black and green letters on our lawn: "*HAVE FAITH. YOU GOT THIS.*" Throughout that year of connection with our community and via *CaringBridge*, we were often reminded of our blessings in love, generosity, and kindness. This helped us to remain grateful and faithful. It's a very humbling experience when you realize how many hands hold you during your most vulnerable moments in life. We can never thank our neighbors, friends, medical staff, community members, and even strangers enough for this. It still keeps us going. Christian initiated a culture of care during his time with us, and his legacy continues to nourish our community with his selfless and nonjudgmental approach. The visible reminders live on.

I would like to add an excerpt from Nancy and Rob's tribute here that reached us after Christian's passing, which is relevant to the rosary prayer meetings. Nancy wrote,

> After we had the first candlelight vigil, I realized that we needed to pray on a more regular basis. I knew your relationship with the Virgin Mary and suggested praying the rosary each week. As you know, I am Protestant, not Catholic, and I had never prayed the rosary before. This type of prayer was totally foreign to me, but with Michele and Cheryl as teachers, I soon realized the power of praying the rosary.
>
> Over the years, you [Danielle] and I have had conversations when we talked about Mother Mary and how, although I prayed to her, Protestants do not specifically pray to her and other saints. However, during our weekly meetings, standing on holy ground outside of your house, I grew closer to the Virgin Mary. Our entire group could feel her presence, God's presence, and the Holy Spirit surrounding you all.
>
> And although we all prayed individually at home, we felt there was power in our prayer when we gathered together. We all felt honored and humbled to be able to lift you all up in prayer. We felt the Holy Spirit moving among us and you all. And although God didn't answer our prayers the way we wished He had, we know that our prayers were answered and that Christian is now rejoicing in heaven, waiting to be reunited with everyone someday.

Danielle and I found the Rosary Gals' prayers very encouraging, and on September 29th, 2020, we wrote the following on the CaringBridge site:

> Once a week, usually on Tuesday at 10 a.m., the wonderful Rosary Gals come and pray the Rosary at our home. I pray it with them inside the house. I'm too teary-eyed these days for public prayer.

Support from family and the community remained strong during October 2020. The Pine Richland Boys Soccer team (Christian's brother, Nicholas, is a member of the team) led a stunning T-shirt promotion project in support of Christian. Christian remained playful, and when asked what he would like to have printed on them, he replied, *"Christian Cochran got cancer and all I got was this lousy T-shirt."* He never lost his quirky sense of humor. We had family days of making pasta and meatballs together with Christian's grandad. We welcomed Daisy June (our new energetic puppy) to brighten up the energy at home. (Christian loved dogs.) We parsed through photos and memories from more carefree days in Prague and Venice together and shared these with our *CaringBridge* community.

Toward the end of our *CaringBridge* journaling, we posted more photos and entries of the good times spent with him, and fewer of our challenges. We intentionally maintained our gratitude for others' support, despite increasingly challenging times for our family. We held on to hope and noticed its signs in the smallest gestures and observations. On two specific occasions, we wrote the following:

> Laughter is the BEST medicine! Smiling is great for you too! Christian has always had a terrific smile and laugh—they light up the room! He smiles and laughs often, even when things aren't perfect.
>
> Quite often, we have wonderful family and friends that deliver all sorts of lovely gifts, cards, food, flowers, books, and more to our home—the thoughtfulness brightens our spirits and truly showers us with God's blessings and love. There are so many AMAZING, LOVING, KIND-HEARTED people in this world!

While we tried to maintain some sense of normality on the domestic front, we had continuous communication with people who were (and still are) actively involved with cancer care and research. We had a good Zoom call with Melinda Bachini and Stacie Lindsey who head up the Cholangiocarcinoma Foundation (www.cholangiocarcinoma.org). They have been amazing advocates for so many and, of course, for our beautiful son. The connection between them and Christian instantly hit a positive note and he had them laughing, even in the most difficult discussions. During their discussions, they explained that so many people dealing with this cancer in the world go through it alone without access to good health care. This was one of the things that Christian wanted to change. He fervently wanted to make a difference by promoting care and kindness in the sense of community support. Toward December, we were guided by Dr. John J. Fung (one of Dr. Starzl's early transplant fellows at the University of Pittsburgh in the 1980s) who led a strong team of medical support right to the end of our journey.

And, of course, throughout these final months of 2020, we had to face our chemotherapy days. We started calling them *"wabi sabi"* or *"kintsugi"* days. On this topic in her journal, Danielle wrote,

> Today is Christian's "wabi sabi" or "kintsugi" day. [Both terms focus primarily on imperfections.] That is what we call chemotherapy days around here (hours of intense drugs flowing into Christian's body—one drug even has platinum in it). Christian has always loved the culture and history of Japan. He is planning on visiting Japan in his future. A few weeks ago, I learned about the ancient art of kintsugi, the 400-year-old technique of repairing something broken, and making it even better! That is what we are doing: taking our sweet Christian and fixing his broken cracks, making him something more beautiful, special, resilient, and unique! I know what you are thinking... He was already ALL of these things and many more.

Christian never complained about his illness, but always looked for and shared the positive things. As mentioned in the journal entry above, he got excited about the fact that the weekly chemotherapy drug he took had platinum in it—he thought that that was "pretty neat." The new drug that was added to his chemo was stronger and more difficult to tolerate—but Christian remained strong...

Friends and family joined us for visits as the year drew to a close. These reunions nourished our souls and gave us joy. All the Cochran cousins came together in support of Christian: strength in numbers! Thanksgiving is always one of our family's favorite holidays of the year. Not only did we share this reunion with our friends and family at the time, but our new golden puppy, Daisy June, joined in as well, following us around, that day and on many others to come. We kept counting and reminding ourselves of our blessings.

One of the moments that stood out before Christmas 2020 was a very special gift from my college wrestling buddies and their families. They sent Christian a pair of unique shoes to wear along his journey. He had a unique retro style as I've mentioned before, and these Nike high tops were spot-on vintage for him. He exclaimed, "Damn, I look fresh as hell in these new shoes!" They were inscribed with the words *"Way Maker"*: one who makes a way, a pioneer, a pathfinder. Christian was making his own way, for sure! He was the most high-spirited, positive, upbeat kiddo I knew. He always had peace in his heart and soul and lived each day with goodness, serenity, and respect. I am still in awe of his beauty and strength. We felt truly blessed to receive such a thoughtful, loving gift from people who had never met our sweet Christian. Just before Christmas Day, our community made us feel more loved and supported:

> There were carolers at our door this evening making joyful music for us, an anonymous kind person sent Christian a coogi sweater [1990s vintage style sweater], which Christian totally "vibes," and I cannot bake Christmas cookies fast enough to keep for tomorrow's Christmas Eve celebrations. We are blessed! We are in a position to see the absolute goodness in people and it brings us such hope and joy! We took our annual Christmas card a week before things dramatically changed our lives. Christian didn't feel well, Kate was leaving for college, and we had tests scheduled to see what was going on with Christian. I told him we did not need to take the photo (I knew he was not up for it) and he said to me, "Mom, I know how much it means to you," and he gladly participated and smiled. He always, always thinks of others first.

Our year came full circle and we ended it in nature with each other: always pleasant and soothing to our souls. We hiked around Deep Creek, MD on cold snowy days and found it a very pleasing way to end the year. In January, we shared some photos on the website of Christian skipping stones. For us, stones are symbols of luck and energy. We kept hoping for both as we entered a new year with Christian's cancer. Christian always loved skipping stones. If there was water nearby, he would always look for stones and skip them. For us, that was a metaphor for the profound ripple effect of Christian's everflowing love. In the Bible, Peter becomes the "rock" that Christ built his church on. (*Petros* translates to "stone.") Christian became that "rock" to our family: skipping stones and sending ripples of love to those who knew him and heard stories of his great love.

At the beginning of 2021, the scan results showed that the treatment was effective, and Christian's doctors (Dr. Fung's team in Chicago, Christian's team at Hillman, Memorial Sloan Kettering, and the NIH) all saw positive signs of healing. We felt deeply guided within this network of brilliant minds. Dr. Jason Luke was recommended by Dr. Fung. He is the director of the Cancer Immunotherapeutics Center within the UPMC Hillman Cancer Immunology Department here in Pittsburgh. We kept moving forward with much to do, a long journey ahead, and many obstacles to overcome in that small world for those who specialized in Christian's cancer. But by March of that year, things took a turn, and we were more and more challenged to remain positive and hopeful. As Danielle wrote in her journal,

> I cannot make any worldly sense of Christian's diagnosis or the path our family is now on. In the blink of an eye, everything changed on August 26th, 2020. All of a sudden, life shifted course and every hope and dream distilled into "Please cure our wonderful Christian." We have become knowledgeable about cholangiocarcinoma as well as genetic mutations that can underlie the disease with the help of a whole team of great doctors and experts consulting and guiding us. Christopher and I have daily conference calls with my sister Bridget and my brother-in-law David, as our family discovers and discusses new paths for Christian's care.

In April, I was asked to speak at the annual World Cholangiocarcinoma Foundation event on my experience as a parent caregiver. We were happy to connect to people all over the world who could share our fears and discoveries as time steadily moved on at its heavy and unchangeable pace. Some of these people were as young as Christian and were reaching out to compare experiences and find mutual hope. Knowledge shared became our strength. We were elated when Christian was finally—after waiting for seven months—accepted into a T-cell trial at the University of Pittsburgh Medical Center (UPMC) in Pittsburgh. We recognized the amazing blessing that befell us of having it in our backyard. The only other medical center in the country that participated in this trial at the time was the National Institute of Health (NIH) in Washington, D.C.—and their trial arm was on hold due to the construction of a new facility. We were hopeful that our "paths may be straightened" again. We were optimistic, and I wrote the following on the CaringBridge site:

> On March 17th, Christian will go in for surgery, which is the first phase of trial participation. We really like his surgeon. He is not only highly competent, but also has a great sense of humor. He and Christian exchanged jokes throughout their recent visit. Once they harvest the T-cells from Christian, following the operation, they will grow an army of good T-cells (TIL) to put back into his body. Hopefully, with a good response, the doctors will then briefly wipe out Christian's immune system with medications and then reintroduce a drastically expanded number of kick-ass cells back into his body to overwhelm the cancer. It's all very "Star Trek-ish" as Christian says! Let's pray and hope that it is successful.
>
> We love the team here in Pittsburgh, headed by Dr. Kammula who started with the TIL trial over a decade ago at the NIH. So, on St. Patrick's Day, Christian—our fine partly Irish young man—will begin another new path on this journey. May St. Patrick and the luck of the Irish be with Christian and us all. "May the road rise up to meet you. May the wind always be at your back. May the sun shine warm upon your face, and rains fall soft upon your fields" [an old Irish blessing].

The day Christian was accepted into the TIL trial marked the beginning of a harrowing countdown.

To participate, he had to halt his chemotherapy for five weeks, allowing the toxins in his body to dissipate fully. During this precarious period, we clung to hope and focused on his well-being: ensuring that he ate nutritiously, took daily walks, and maintained a positive outlook (buoyed by prayer). This waiting game intensified when we learned that we had to wait an additional four weeks to determine if the T-cells would thrive in the lab. Every passing day felt like a weighty burden and as a family, we held our collective breath in eager anticipation. We clung to the thought that his surgery date coincided with St. Patrick's Day: the subtle whisper of hope and nudge of something divine.

On the morning of the surgery, Danielle told me of a vision she had, which she also captured in extraordinary detail in her journal. I believe sharing her exact words may show the weight of our emotions at the time. I believe, too, that our family witnessed a divine intervention:

> I woke up early in the morning to my son and his father getting ready to leave for the hospital. It was still dark outside. It was the much anticipated morning of our beloved Christian's T-cell trial. We had put all our hopes and prayers into this trial—we truly felt it would work and we would be able to save our dear son.
>
> When I woke, I was overwhelmed with a sense of calm, peace, and hope that the operation was going to be a success. I sat up in my bed and told them that I just experienced the most amazing dream—with images of places in the vast universe that I had never experienced. I was with the Blessed Mother, and she was showing me the glorious universe: It was so vast and the stars and planets sparkled brightly against a deep blue sapphire sky. My favorite color, blue, was all around me, embracing us.
>
> The stars were life-like, as if they had souls and were loving and familiar to me. They were brighter than anything I have ever witnessed from Earth, yet they did not hurt my sight. I felt the presence of my father who recently died, my grandparents, and many people that I loved who had recently passed.
>
> The Blessed Mother was controlling the visual spectacle that I was watching. It was put there for me to see—she wanted me to experience it, as if she was the conductor of a symphony of stars and planets dancing and swirling about in the universe. It was like an orchestra meeting its crescendo: a dazzling sight to behold. Everything in front of my eyes were all moving in their destined directions without direct projection, sparkling brightly along the way. It was a perfect artful display in its completeness.

I was mesmerized by the spectacular visual show playing out before my eyes. I became a part of it, in the presence of the Blessed Mother who took me there to show me that everything would be okay and that Christian was going to be fine. For the first time since his diagnosis, I felt relaxed. I felt some worry dissipate and I remained full of hope that entire day.

As Christian and his father left for the hospital, I kissed them both, and told them about my vision. Throughout the day, I remained excited and filled with hope. I told my sister, when I met her later that day to attend prayers at the St. Patrick's Church, that Christian was going to be fine. I said to her that the Blessed Mother took me there, where she showed me the most glorious display of dancing stars that I have ever witnessed, to tell me that our son was going to be okay.

I realize today, three years and one day later, that the Blessed Mother revealed a glimpse of heaven to me. She showed me the celestial sky—something that Christian loved very much and studied regularly. She allowed me a brief glimpse of heaven at that moment in time to feel the greatest profound love: free of worry, sadness, and pain. As a mother, she wanted me to see this and feel it so that I would know that Christian would be fine. She revealed that he would be with her, the angels, his family, and all the other family members that went before us. The dream assured me that he would be somewhere glorious: a place that no one had seen. She shared God's creation and it was truly a snippet of the beauty and glory of God. Through this revelation, I came to understand that perhaps that was the journey my sweet Christian took. I'm sad he had to travel alone. I wish it was me going before him or being with him. A mother always wants to protect and know that her children are safe and happy

As we made our way to UPMC Shadyside in Pittsburgh for the surgery, my wife took solace and strength in the oldest church in the city, St. Patrick's Church. Nestled in the heart of the bustling Strip District, its historical significance mirrored the weight of our prayers. Meanwhile, Christian—always the beacon of light—charmed every member of the surgical team with his infectious humor and genuine warmth. His ability to turn strangers into friends with a simple greeting was nothing short of miraculous.

I vividly recall the moments before the surgery, seeking refuge in the hospital chapel, my pleas to a higher power intermingling with tears of desperation. I bargained with God, promising my soul in exchange for Christian's healing, a desperate plea echoed by my wife as well throughout our journey. In those sacred moments, faith mingled with fear and hope intertwined with uncertainty.

The surgery went as expected. The team managed to skillfully get the tissue needed for the T-cell cultivation. And so, the countdown resumed: a silent clock ticking away the precious days as we waited for news of the T-cell's viability. The cutting-edge treatment represented more than just a chance at remission for Christian; it symbolized progress, innovation, and the promise of a higher future for countless others battling cancer. This is how Christian saw that moment in time.

Christian embraced the journey not only as a fight for his survival but as a crusade for the greater good. He saw beyond his pain, finding solace in the belief that the ordeal could pave the way for future breakthroughs in medicine. His altruistic, unwavering commitment to making a difference served as a beam of inspiration for us all. Amid uncertainty, we found strength. In the face of adversity, we discovered resilience. And in Christian's unwavering spirit, we witnessed the transformative power of love, hope, and selflessness. My journal entry from that day (March 17th, 2021) is as follows:

> I have not written for some time but today is another big day in the life of Christian. Today marks the fifth week since he has been off chemo. He was accepted into the TIL trial, which we have been targeting for some time and could never get in before now! Today is an important part of the "puzzle"—when they will be extracting two to three lymph node tumors. We hope to get all three tumors in his shoulder, but it's more likely to get less. From there, they will extract T-cells to save his life.
>
> Watching my beautiful son getting wheeled back for major surgery like this plays heavy tricks on my mind while at the same time providing a positive hope for a cure. Still, it remains

only one step ahead of the many steps we have to face. I pray that this could cure him. I pray that this is successful and that we are on the right track.

I love to watch Christian work a room: He has that thing that so many people (including me) wish they had. The way of making everyone around him feel comfortable. He makes them laugh and truly knows how to connect with anyone.

He is so destined to be successful at changing the world!

Needless to say, our resilience was continuously tested as we awaited updates from the medical team in the laboratory. My frequent calls did not help my patience... During this tense waiting period, I dedicated my energy to becoming increasingly informed about my son's life-threatening illness. I immersed myself in research and connecting with others who might offer insights to overcoming this challenge. Rest was foreign to me, as sleeping seemed like a waste of precious time that could be spent learning.

As time pressed on, we faced an additional anxious five-week waiting period to confirm the effectiveness of the T-cells, resulting in over two months without chemotherapy. On April 29th, I was scheduled to visit Indiana University of Pennsylvania with my younger son, Nicholas. It was a significant day, as Nick decided to attend the same university that Christian had graduated from and where his sister, Kate, was enrolled. After an almost two-hour drive, we were joined by Kate when we arrived around midday, ready and excited about the anticipated campus tour.

During our reunion, my phone rang with a call from the doctor at the TIL trial. As I stepped aside to take the call, I received the disheartening news: "Christian's T-cells are not proliferating sufficiently; they're too weak. Regrettably, he must exit the trial." I watched Nicholas and Kate sharing a joyful moment as the weight of the news hit me profoundly. A sensation of dread was soon overwhelming me. I immediately called Danielle and together we sprang into action, coordinating with the healthcare team to ensure Christian could start chemotherapy again the following day.

From the moment we learned of Christian's diagnosis until the very end, we tirelessly sought solutions with the help of the family—in particular with Danielle's sister, Bridget, and her husband, David. Christian entrusted his health with us, often deferring to our judgment with a simple, "Whatever you guys think is best." We bore this tremendous responsibility, hoping to ease Christian's burden in any way possible. In pursuit of answers, we explored in-depth genetic testing of Christian's DNA and RNA, hoping to uncover a key to his recovery.

Our journey subsequently took a new direction: Our determination to seek medical options remained unwavering. Christian received care from specialists scattered across the US, all familiar with his battle. We consulted with top experts in the field of cholangiocarcinoma at renowned institutions such as MD Anderson in Texas, Mass General in Boston, the Cleveland Clinic in Cleveland, Sloan Kettering in NYC, University of Chicago in Chicago, and Johns Hopkins in Baltimore.

From the outset, we advocated relentlessly for molecular testing at facilities nationwide, hoping to identify a genetic mutation that could offer Christian a lifeline. Despite frequently facing disheartening updates, our quest remained singular: to find the FGFR2 mutation, a potential game-changer. Fibroblast growth factor receptors (FGFR) are proteins that assist normal growth and division of cells. Some patients (very few) with bile duct cancers show abnormal FGFR protein growth that turns into cancer. According to an article in the National Library of Medicine, "Cholangiocarcinomas (CCAs) are rare but aggressive tumors with poor diagnosis and limited treatment options." The researchers elaborate in the article that, "FGFR inhibitors have become an integral part of CCA treatment" (Chmiel et al., 2022, para 1, 21, 25, 26) and, furthermore, that:

> The occurrence of CCA is mainly associated with the mutations that lead to the upregulation of the FGF/FGFR signaling pathway. Thus, researchers continuously strive to develop such inhibitors and targeted therapies that would specifically inhibit the carcinogenic effects of this disturbed pathway.

In essence, FGFR inhibitors allow for a breakthrough of favorable outcomes in the treatment of various cancers, especially cholangiocarcinoma.

Our perseverance paid off in May, during a consultation at Johns Hopkins where we received the breakthrough news that this mutation had recently been identified and approved for use. This discovery meant that Christian could begin treatment with Pemazyre, a daily medication that had demonstrated effectiveness in patients with intrahepatic cholangiocarcinoma. (It blocks the abnormal FGFR2 protein and may prevent cancer cells from growing, or may even destroy them.) We embarked on a frantic race to obtain this medicine, navigating a maze of bureaucratic obstacles under the pressure of time. Despite the constant challenges and the acute awareness that time was slipping away, our resolve to do everything possible for Christian's survival never diminished. Unfortunately, this path also fell apart once we saw Christian's newest CT scans.

After the disappointment of the T-cell trial, the prolonged absence of chemotherapy, and multiple trials failing—our beloved son's cancer had metastasized further. It was spreading aggressively throughout his body, particularly targeting his bones and spine. The burden of pain weighed heavily on him, necessitating three back surgeries. The memory of the last remains the most vivid: Both Danielle and I stood by him at the Shadyside Hospital and as the procedure concluded, I fetched the car, leaving them to a quiet moment of solace. Upon returning, I found the two in the hospital room—an aura of tranquility enveloping them. Christian rested his head upon Danielle's shoulder, their hands intertwined in a silent bond of love and comfort. The room seemed to hold its breath—their presence the only solace in the stillness of the evening. In that poignant moment, my mind drifted back in time with a stark juxtaposition of past and present. Almost 23 years earlier, I had held Christian in this very hospital. His worldly arrival was a signal of hope and joy. The memories flooded back: Danielle cradling our newborn son, the overwhelming pride, and the gratitude of fatherhood.

But the present reality pierced through that nostalgic haze—a stark reminder of the cruel twist of fate being dealt. Where once there was celebration, now stood the somber struggle to save our son. Still, amid the emotional turmoil, I couldn't help but marvel at the profound connection between Danielle and Christian. Their love transcended words, an unspoken bond forged through years of shared moments and unwavering support. In that hospital room, their closeness was palpable—a testament to the enduring strength of their relationship. Christian, with his eyes closed in exhaustion, mirrored the peaceful innocence of his newborn self nestled against Danielle's shoulder.

Their tenderly profound bond illuminated the room with a warmth that defied the chill of despair. At that moment, I realized that the treasures of the heart outweigh any material wealth. The sight of Danielle and Christian together, united in love and resilience, was a symbol of the enduring power of familial love.

Throughout Christian's arduous journey with cancer, he consistently urged his doctors to utilize his body for any necessary testing aimed at advancing knowledge of discovering a cure. Christian's innate desire to be of service to others was a defining characteristic of his. He viewed his struggle not solely as a personal ordeal but as an opportunity to contribute to a higher cause. The selflessness was deeply ingrained in his ethos, guiding his actions throughout his life. He demonstrated an unwavering willingness to make sacrifices for the well-being of others, driven by a profound sense of love and compassion.

Christian's altruistic nature was palpable in his interactions with the medical team. I vividly recall him expressing his willingness to donate his body to science to his oncologist, Dr. Raj, as his journey neared its end. With humility and gratitude, Dr. Raj acknowledged Christian's noble offer and assured him that his contributions had already been valuable. In Dr. Raj's gentle words, Christian found solace, knowing that his selfless efforts had left an indelible mark on the quest for a cure.

During these last few months of his life, our primary focus remained on caring for our son. *CaringBridge* updates took a step back while our emotions became more pronounced. In every gesture, and in every conversation, Christian's sincere dedication to serving others shone brightly. His legacy of compassion and generosity continues to inspire us, reminding us of the deep-seated impact one individual can have on the world by simply finding purpose in living with an open heart and a willingness to give oneself for a higher good.

Danielle and I prayed every minute of every day for a miracle once Christian was diagnosed—we were desperate for one. And we thought we would get one. The thing is, we didn't understand the concept of a miracle until he left us. It's only now, reflecting on Christian's beauty, that we realize we got our miracle: We were blessed to be the parents of Christian Anthony Cochran. We were blessed for 23 years—and perhaps blessed most profoundly in the last year of Christian's life, as we watched him accept his destiny with such humility, love, grace, and peace.

[Please note that liberty has been taken with grammatical changes to the *CaringBridge* reflections for improved readability.] (CaringBridge, 2022).

# Embracing Spirituality

Christian embraced an eclectic spiritual journey incorporating elements from different religions. He was keenly interested in and admired various spiritual philosophies that demonstrate a shared wisdom and compassion. As such, apart from practicing his strong Catholic faith, he was willing to learn from diverse spiritual sources. One of these was Taoism, which places a high value on life. (Specifically maintaining focus on having a life well lived.) Tao followers see life and death as an inseparable wholeness. Death is simply a process toward a different dimension or another phase in life. It's often defined by the opposing ideas of being and nonbeing. Christian's life exemplified this strong focus on living a healthy life based on simplicity and inner peace, as true Tao followers aim to do, without fearing death.

Although he was raised in the Catholic faith, he also delved deeper into Judaism and intimately explored the Christian Bible. Apart from Taoist texts, Christian furthermore enjoyed reading the works of Rumi and navigated Muslim and Buddhist sources to find deeper meaning. Having this open-mindedness about spirituality and the diverse religions within enriched his worldview and, in my opinion, offered him a broader perspective on kindness and compassion.

## *Navigating Loss Faithfully*

Many have asked about our faith in the aftermath of losing our son. To be honest, it was profoundly shaken to its core. I journeyed from anger toward God to a deep sense of disappointment, which has been incredibly challenging. Grief is universal, but losing a child surpasses all forms of grief, leaving one utterly debilitated and questioning the very fabric of existence. It becomes a constant companion, clinging relentlessly, shaping every moment of every day.

Danielle was confronted in her own unique way with the harrowing reality of losing a child. Throughout her faithful existence, she has experienced daily expressions of gratitude for the countless blessings bestowed graciously upon her life. Her journey has often led her to the sacred stillness of churches, and the peaceful moments spent in prayer have always been highly cherished. This is a legacy she inherited from her youth, and she grew up to share it in the loving company of her family and children. That profound spiritual connection deepened the shock when she learned of our beloved Christian's rare and incurable cancer. Before this, her faith in God had served as the bedrock for her way of viewing life.

Confronted with this harrowing reality, questions stormed her heart: Why *my* child? Why *us*? Danielle has shared with me that her dedication to God had always been unwavering: She nurtured her children in a spirit of kindness and compassion, embodying God's teachings. Yet, facing this trial cast her into an abyss of sorrow and helplessness, the likes of which she had never before encountered. It was a poignant reminder of her vulnerability, of the illusion of control she had over life's narrative, and the realization that even her fervent prayers could not sway the journey that God had ordained for our son.

Amid this turmoil, feelings of abandonment and despair threatened to overshadow our faith, as if it had been left alone by a once-intimate ally. Yet, through the anguish, I've begun to perceive life as a tapestry woven with threads of perspective. I feel compelled to believe that

Christian's pain and suffering must serve a greater purpose—something remarkable and good. In seeking solace through our priest, we were bestowed with a profound reassurance: God welcomes our anger, and shares in our grief, desiring to connect with us even as we traverse our deepest valleys of doubt and suffering.

In our journey, we've chosen to embrace action, echoing Christian's unwavering question, *what's good about today*? His legacy motivates us to seek goodness in every moment, to cherish beauty amid pain, and to find solace in the enduring bonds of love that transcend earthly limits. Danielle told me that this tempest has illuminated the incredible privilege bestowed upon us, in particular to her as a mother. His 23 years on Earth were a gift, enriching our lives with immeasurable love and happiness: treasures to be cherished eternally.

Our relationship with God is intricate, much like any human relationship, encompassing a spectrum of emotions—joy, sadness, anger, pain, despair, resilience, hope, peace, and action. Ultimately, we maintain our relationship with God and remain steadfast in our faith. God and His promises are integral to our lives. Though our faith may tremble in the face of adversity, we remain humble and loving toward God, committed to honoring Christian's memory by embodying his message of hope, resilience, and unwavering faith in the goodness of each day. As a family, our ultimate desire is to reunite in heaven for eternity. We do not fear death, knowing it marks the beginning of a new life with our beloved Christian. We hope he awaits us as we embark on the greatest journey of our lives, God willing. I share his mother's loving words here with you:

> While I long for the day we will be reunited in heavens' embrace, I find solace in the belief that God entrusted me with the sacred duty of nurturing Christian's soul: a task I embraced with love and honor. Through his journey, my heart has been drawn closer to God, finding peace in his divine plan and the everlasting promise of his love and mercy.

Bruce Lee said, "Do not pray for an easy life, pray for the strength to endure a difficult one" (Quotefancy, n.d.-a). During our family's challenging journey, this quote often came to mind as we faced every new day's obstacles. Regardless of your choice in prayers, we have seen that a higher spirit guides us in our faith. Faithful praying is a collective strength, regardless of your deity of choice. We observed Christian's spiritual vantage point and we learned from that: The cancer journey wasn't easy at all. But in the name of love, acceptance, and gratitude, our family made it through, despite the devastating loss and pain.

## Concluding Thoughts: Inspired by Christian

To impel change, we have to pause and reflect first. There is power in pausing: it is the ability to be mindful of every moment and take in what life presents us with. Christian was a master of mindfulness.

- Remain graceful on any journey. The essence of life can be found in small mundane things. Encourage others to find the *good in today*. Observe your blessings.

- Support others during difficulties. Be there for them. Hold them. Find joy in hardships. Embrace imperfections. Be kind.

- Hold on to your faith in adverse conditions. Find the benefits of belonging to a community. There is strength in numbers.

- Remain mindful. Steer clear from ruminating about the past or the future. Be fully present. The art of pausing opens our eyes to the beauty around us.

- Touch a life. Make a change. Don't be consumed by regrets.

- Learn to trust loved ones. Learn to let go. Learn to flow.

- Remind yourself of the ripple effect of love.

- Find gratitude in any obstacle. Always keep on dancing.

# Chapter 3:

# Christian's Tao

*The softest thing in the world dashes against and overcomes the hardest; that which has no (substantial) existence enters where there is no crevice. I know hereby what advantage belongs to doing nothing (with a purpose).* –Lao Tzu

Few people understand the value of nonaction (or effortless action, called *wu wei*), a prominent Tao concept. Even though many questions surround the mysterious life of the ancient philosopher Lao Tzu and his teachings, it is believed that his words have inspired many since the fifth and sixth centuries BC. A contemporary of Confucius, Lao Tzu's *Tao Te Ching* is considered a masterpiece and forms the main work of the Tao philosophy. Following the flow of the *Wu-Wei* enables a person to avoid extremes, worries, and ruminations.

What makes the Tao concept so difficult to comprehend (often in Western societies) is the fact that every individual has the ability to obtain the Tao *on their own terms*. For many religions and societies, this concept is quite foreign, and a more concrete definition is often sought. Tao philosophers continue to explain that Tao is a force beyond our comprehension that cannot be perceived by our senses. They agree that Tao is merely the harmonious ability to live in agreement with the flow, and not to question it.

## The Taoist Way: Going With the Flow

Christian's Taoist views influenced his outlook on life and also his attitude toward his diagnosis. In Tao philosophy—the philosophy of flow—we break complications down by quieting the overactive brain. When we think back to major scientific discoveries in the past, we realize that moments of great enlightenment often arose in moments of "doing nothing." Think of Newton's life-changing gravitation theory which developed from the simple act of an apple falling from an overhanging tree branch. Observing this simple yet detailed moment in time—in such a moment of quiet—helped spur on one of the greatest discoveries of mankind: gravitational pull.

Tao philosophy focuses mainly on such quiet and mindful observations in the present moment. And as it does so, it attempts to silence the constant chattering that we all experience in our heads. In the words of mental health and mindfulness advocate Wayne O'Toole, "Some of the biggest things in life are found in moments of 'nothing'" (2021, para 5). In Taoism, life is compared to the flow of a river. It doesn't offer resistance to the natural ebb and flow that comes with obstacles on its course. Instead, it is merely believed that the river already has its set course, and that calm comes from following its natural flow.

The problem arises when humans think they have options in this river metaphor. When we think we can swim against the current, or hold on to a branch and wait, we impose our human nature on the Tao. This analogy portrays the human fallacy of thinking that we can control the flow or current! As soon as we realize that we cannot control everything and that such control is not a prerequisite for survival (in fact, it can worsen or hamper our struggle to survive), we embrace a calmness that helps us flow with the river and navigate the challenges in a more tranquil manner. Only then can we let go and follow the natural flow of the stream—the flow of *life*.

Now, I don't think that Christian ever thought about this in such detail, as he instinctively portrayed these virtues in life starting from an early age. Even though he always had a keen interest in Eastern philosophies, he merely followed what made sense to him and what felt "normal" to him. Many of us, unfortunately, do not have that same inherent intuition and we keep fighting and struggling while we deny the gentle flow of circumstances. Christian accepted his plight when he learned of his cancer diagnosis. As with the Tao water analogy, he remained gentle and humble. He didn't swim against the current.

We can learn from his example: When faced with one of the most challenging obstacles, he did not fight it. He humbly accepted what was part of his "set course" on this Earth. His gentle and kind nature helped him understand that it was not death that had to be feared, it was the suffering of others—especially loved ones who had to be soothed. Throughout his post-diagnosis journey, he managed to shift his approach (within its natural flow) to help his loved ones reduce their pain. He had already made peace with his journey, but his loved ones hadn't. This became his primary focus as he navigated that river of change.

## Learning From All Walks of Life

So, how do we go with the flow as the Tao guides us? There is no one particular clue to this, and it certainly does not imply that we should sit down and close our eyes and do nothing! To achieve such stillness of mind (our *yin*), we can abstain from constantly striving, we can remain humble, and we can curb our senses to open us up for the natural flow of things.

Taoist philosophy also adds a component of softness and humility through the water analogy. These concepts are Taoist virtues: humility and kindness as opposed to fighting or resisting the natural flow. Resistance is seen as an egotistical ignorance of reality. (We cannot change reality...) The Tao is gentleness. Gentleness is represented by the water, which is nourishing and yielding. It overcomes hardness (rocks) through the gentleness of its flow. Water has no specific desire or goal—it merely flows.

Of course, we can rush and get things done forcibly, but does that truly enhance our livelihood and peace of mind? We end up spending so much time and energy in the process that we may end up with collateral damage. And what's the point of that? According to the Tao, a wise person approaches everything in a harmoniously balanced way between action and nonaction; anxiety and boredom...

This is in stark contrast to Western beliefs that prescribe ambition, control, and egotistical striving. The collateral damage of these beliefs are psychoses such as depression, anxiety and sleep disorders, aggression, addiction, burnout, and a range of things that we then have to try and cure. Western culture often looks down upon passivity. Let's consider this for a moment: Many problems actually solve themselves! According to Roopak Mahadane in his Medium post on Tao (Mahadane, 2019, para 11),

> When we look at nature, "doing nothing" makes way more sense than we tend to think. Results do not equal the amount of energy we spend. Results are the consequences of a series of actions. [Much] of this action comes naturally and a task doesn't need more human intervention than necessary to steer it into the right direction.

Tao shows us how to navigate the river, not to resist its flow. Being in a state of flow removes the repercussions from the past, the pressures from the present moment, and the anticipated anxieties of the future. It means letting go and living with our *wu wei*.

Christian was curious about different cultures and perspectives. He knew he could learn something from everybody. For him, it was important to have friends from different walks of life, so they could learn from each other and come together in harmony, peace, and love. He found people's differences interesting and remained curious about them. In this virtue of constantly desiring to discover more, he was always learning and improving his knowledge. He embraced an open-minded approach to his spiritual beliefs. This meant living his life—while being a practicing Catholic—with some elements from other religious inclinations and spiritual philosophies. Christianity and Buddhism share many similarities. Christian was well aware of this. He placed a high value on some of these similar concepts, and chiefly among them was the importance of love and honesty.

He harnessed the most beautiful aspects of all of these and made them his own. He lived them through his example, more than preaching any particular one or being overly religious. His focus remained inclusive, respectful, and spiritual.

He was a devoted minimalist (as in the Buddhist philosophy). He would joke about having to drive our fancy cars. Instead, he preferred his old and slightly worn-out Honda. His thrifting attitude toward life underscored his uncomplicated and nonmaterialistic nature: Again, he loved anything retro. And more importantly, he valued experiences and relationships over any material possessions.

He was always at peace in his heart and in his mind. He remained grateful for all things. This enhanced his inner peace and feelings of comfort in his own skin, as so many have said about him. He never failed to be authentically himself.

When Christian entered college, he decided to read the Bible from beginning to end. Back when he had been a young boy, he would read the Bible to his dog, Lula, to ensure that she would one day make it to heaven. He read all the time, in fact, developing his curiosity about the world and its people. He had a rich and brilliant mind, developed from a young age and it stayed with him.

He suffered his burden for God and for the conversion of others. We've had countless testimonials from people all over the world who shared how Christian profoundly touched and altered their lives. Indeed, he was always present when he was with others: His actions and words were intentionally meaningful and lovingly sincere. These actions of his were habitual and repeated to anyone he encountered.

Christian was a true Taoist soul lost in a fractured world. He chose to follow the course of the river and he didn't resist. His inherent being helped others to find the light. And his virtues still guide us. Until today, the ripple effect of his love is ever-flowing, just as Tao philosophy encourages us to go with the flow instead of swim upstream.

Through all the spiritual walks of life that Christian harnessed, what stands out the most to me is how he refrained from forcing them onto others. He simply lived his life as an example of these saintly virtues. He made them visible to us through his unique ways.

# Love, Courage, Kindness

Christian represented strength. In less than two weeks after his diagnosis, he'd courageously made peace with it. He never complained about his pain. Instead, he characteristically showed only kindness and love for others. His main worry was the prospect of his family having to watch as their loved one slowly died before them. As a result, he took a job to set an example to his siblings: showing them that he was moving forward.

He applied to graduate school, wrote a brilliant essay (which I discuss further in Chapter 4), and presented ideas from his essay in a speech he delivered to the Cholangiocarcinoma Foundation (CCF). He also searched for and found a beautiful apartment to live in, continued creating his digital music on SoundCloud, and started a new podcast with friends. Christian loved his music and dancing and continued to create and celebrate. He used to listen to jazz when going in for radiation treatments (he would ask his medical personnel to play it for him), and found himself a cool 1980s Walkman so he could be surrounded by music all the time. Christian never stopped living his life.

At the time of his rare diagnosis, another young cholangiocarcinoma patient, Georgia, discovered our story via the Cholangiocarcinoma Foundation. The foundation was aware of the rarity of the diagnosis at such a tender age and informed her mother, Laurie, that there was another person in the States with the same illness, of the same age— that being our sweet Christian. They also lived in Pennsylvania, as it turned out, but on the eastern side of the state.

We made contact, and Laurie confirmed that her daughter had been diagnosed in the same month as Christian. She was finding it very challenging to locate the most suitable medical answers for her daughter's suffering, and so I guided her with some ideas. I got her connected to other doctors and to the broader cholangiocarcinoma world in general. She found solace in the guidance my family was able to offer hers, and from then on, we shared resources and experiences as parents of terminally ill children. However, Georgia wasn't keen on treatments and refused some of the medical things that Christian didn't mind doing. She was in extreme pain, though, and it was Christian who encouraged her to get help to manage it.

Upon learning of Georgia's plight, Christian reached out to her without hesitation, initiating a bond that would become forged in mutual understanding and resilience. Through texts and shared experiences, they became invaluable members of each other's support system, navigating their treatments with hope and courage. Christian, with his unwavering optimism, became a light in Georgia's journey, encouraging her to persevere and seek comfort in treatments that might ease her burden. Their friendship, though they never met in person, was profound, as they offered unique solace only they could provide to one another. They were going through this together. He coached her throughout her entire illness.

When Georgia's journey prematurely ended, five months before his own, the news was heartbreaking to Christian—losing the one person who truly comprehended his struggle. Their story, a testament to the human capacity to connect and uplift, underscores how purposeful our universe truly is. Laurie, Georgia's mother, encapsulated Christian's essence beautifully and recognized his extraordinary empathy and support.

How ironic that two bright young souls—getting ready to venture out into the world after both recently graduating—were both living in the same state, at the same age, and with the same rare illness. (It turned out that Georgia and Christian's girlfriend, Rachael, had even graduated from the same university...) Despite his personal battle, Christian's kindness and bravery shone brightly in their connection: a poignant picture of a young man touching lives with the purity of his spirit. He embodied the very essence of compassion and love even in the face of life's cruelest challenges.

## *Christian's Favorites*

Christian was ahead of his time when he was young in many ways. He wanted to be funny, and jokes were everything to him. He spent a lot of time crafting his own jokes and ideas for the enjoyment of others.

Ironically, he thought of himself as an introvert. In January 2021, I noted some thoughts in my journal about the things that Christian loved. These describe his humble free-spirited, yet whimsical character so well:

>Christian loves:
>
>>House music.
>>
>>Playing video games.
>>
>>Carbonated beverages.
>>
>>History.
>>
>>Praha (Prague).
>>
>>Kendama (a traditional Japanese wooden skill toy with cups, a handle, and a ball).
>>
>>Space and astrology.
>>
>>His dogs (He loves watching them play together, and watching them enjoy life).
>>
>>Vintage computers.
>>
>>Airports—he could live in them.
>>
>>His girlfriend, Rachael.
>>
>>His friends (He misses seeing them so much).
>>
>>Family.
>>
>>Peeling the plastic cover off things, like computer covers.
>>
>>Music over silence.
>>
>>To discover a new song.

Transportation—seeing a plane, boat, or train.

A hot shower.

The internet culture—but hates it too.

He wishes it was always fall and loves camping so much. He loves being in a tent, sitting around a campfire, and drinking Miller High Life.

He loves when people admit they are wrong for the sake of peace.

He loves to make people look good.

He loves talking positively about people, just as much when they're not around him.

He has so much fun making jokes. Anything funny to him—which he knows will make others laugh—means everything to him.

In a world governed by the relentless ticking of the clock, my son lived a different measure of time. At 22 years of age, Christian's calendar wasn't marked by days or months, but by moments of joy, acts of kindness, and the pursuit of meaning. This "different way of keeping time" became his most profound legacy, transforming not only how he lived but also how those around him perceived life.

His timekeeping was unconventional—each moment held the potential for eternity, and each interaction was significant. He understood that life's value wasn't its length but its depth. At his young age, he mastered what many spend a lifetime seeking: the art of living fully in the present, cherishing every encounter, every laugh, and every tear as if they were the very essence of life.

This perspective on time taught us that the moments we overlook are the ones that give life its richest color. It's not the milestones or the number of candles on a birthday cake that define our existence, but the small everyday experiences and love that we share. He showed us that time, in its traditional sense, is a limited currency. But the moments that touch our souls—those are infinite.

Writing about his "different way of keeping time" is not just an act of remembrance—it's a lesson in living. It's a call to shift our gaze from the ticking clock and to start measuring our lives in the smiles we share, the comfort we provide, and the love we spread. It's a testament to the fact that even the shortest lives can leave the most lasting impressions, teaching us that the real essence of time is not in its passing, but in what we do with it.

His legacy challenges us to reconsider our own relationship with time. To count it not in years but in moments of authentic human connection, instances of real joy, and acts of spontaneous kindness. In sharing his story, I hope to inspire others to embrace this enriching perspective on life, ensuring that his way of counting time—so beautiful, so precious—continues to resonate with and inspire others, long after his own time has passed.

## Concluding Thoughts

I quote these wise words from the Tao Te Ching, Chapter 33:

> He who knows other men is discerning; he who knows himself is intelligent. He who overcomes others is strong; he who overcomes himself is mighty. He who is satisfied with his lot is rich; he who goes on acting with energy has a (firm) will.
>
> He who does not fail in the requirements of his position, continues long; he who dies and yet does not perish, has longevity.(Tzu, 2001)

Another translation of Lao Tzu's words is as follows:

> Those who understand others are intelligent
>
> Those who understand themselves are enlightened

Those who overcome others have strength

Those who overcome themselves are powerful

Those who know contentment are wealthy

Those who proceed vigorously have willpower

Those who do not lose their base endure

Those who die but do not perish have longevity (Singh, 2024)

## Concluding Thoughts: Inspired by Christian

The Tao of Christian is a quiet reminder to all of us to stop resisting and start living.

- Don't question the flow. The river already follows its course. Do not resist that. Simply navigate. Trust your sense to embrace the natural flow of things.

- Take effortless action. Stay present in the moment.

- Be open to all walks of life. Respect instead of judge.

- Teach through example, not words.

- How do you count time? Value time in moments of authentic human connection. Value experiences and relationships.

- The value of life can be found in its depth, not in its length. Continue to live your life fully.

# Chapter 4:

# The Role Model

*But I have heard that he who is skillful in managing the life entrusted to him for a time travels on the land without having to shun rhinoceros or tiger, and enters a host without having to avoid buff coat or sharp weapon. The rhinoceros finds no place in him into which to thrust its horn, nor the tiger a place in which to fix its claws, nor the weapon a place to admit its point. And for what reason? Because there is in him no place of death.* –Lao Tzu

Christian was an everlasting role model to many during his time on Earth.

## A Role Model for Many

Christian was asked by the Cholangiocarcinoma Foundation (CCF) to reach out to other newly diagnosed young adults and help them cope with their devastating diagnosis. He was also asked by Young Adult Survivors United (YASU) to be an ambassador of hope to other young adults facing a cancer diagnosis. All of this was because of his uniquely positive, hopeful, happy demeanor that these groups recognized could truly help others who were struggling to cope. He spoke virtually at the CCF annual event on June 4th, 2021. In his speech, Christian shared details that reflected his determination to personally work toward making a difference in the lives of people afflicted with cancer in third-world nations who lack the resources that he had access to. Christian also shared his thoughts, goals, and vision in his application for the Indiana University of Pennsylvania Graduate Studies Program. I am honored to share his brilliant message with you, as follows:

> In my four years at the Indiana University of Pennsylvania, I engaged in a journey that many young adults in this country do.

Certainly, my experience was distinct and my own, but I felt intertwined with the spirit of my generation, to shape the world and have conversations about what we wanted the future to look like. Graduating and jumping off the springboard into adulthood, I had abstract goals and unbridled energy, and I was preparing to head to the West Coast in order to start my life as I had envisioned it up until that point.

Things, of course, progressed differently, and I am sure that I don't need to tell you exactly how my [COVID-19] pandemic has played out. I was incredibly lucky to be hired for a full-time position in Pittsburgh at the start of the pandemic, was excited to have an opportunity to build for my future, and to have the opportunity for introspection that the pandemic (like it or not) provided. While I was still an IUP student, at a Model NATO conference in February of 2020, I noticed that I wasn't feeling myself. What began as me merely not feeling as hungry or energetic as I once did led to me losing nearly 30 pounds by July, and pain that continued to worsen and showed no sign of stopping. On August 26th, I was diagnosed with liver cancer, which after biopsy turned out to be cholangiocarcinoma: a cancer of the bile ducts.

There are many feelings I can associate with what happened to me. It's a period of my life that is still ongoing, fairly fresh, and recent; but it can also feel like an experience that's millions of miles away from me right now. Regardless of the many negative aspects of a serious cancer diagnosis, allow me to present a notable positive one.

I have, at the young age of 22, been given a peculiar opportunity to examine my life in an objective view. I am forced to come to terms with the many aspects that make up my person, both in my internal struggles and my outward desires. I do not intend to imply that cancer has given me some sort of new sense of self, but rather that it has allowed me to feel vulnerable and evaluate what is important to me. That is why you are finding this goal statement today.

Through so much of my life, I have wrapped my identity and interests in history, humanity, and the rich fabric of our collective society. Coming to IUP as an undergrad, I knew I not only wanted to understand the past that brought us to where we are today, but to play an active role in shaping the future that future generations would inherit. I was given by my professors a set of tools in which I could deconstruct and better understand the world. I was given by my peers a tapestry of experiences and interactions that could provide context and new realizations to cultural misunderstandings and societal presumptions. When I left IUP in May 2020, I understood that these concepts would come in handy, but I was then unsure of how I could wield them to affect change in a meaningful way.

Cholangiocarcinoma is a rare and often aggressive form of cancer. With that mixture of rarity and urgency, I have become greatly connected over the past few months with a number of fellow sufferers of this disease, and also acquainted with the bureaucratic mechanisms that help to fund research, spread awareness, and help counsel and assist people with this condition.

I want to take the global worldview that majoring in International Studies has given me and utilize it in a concise and effective manner to bring meaningful change to issues that affect all people. Cholangiocarcinoma will affect me until the end of my life, in one way or another, but it is the lives of others that I am more concerned about.

Currently, cholangiocarcinoma is uncommon in the developed world, but exceedingly common in Southeast Asia. As someone who has spent time in this region of the world, as well as someone who has minored in Asian Studies, I am acutely aware of the wide-ranging economic and infrastructural disparities that exist within. As someone who is also becoming familiar with the complexities of cancer treatment, I am particularly interested in the intersection of these two concepts. I believe that, for me to receive experimental and expensive treatments while others suffer from onset to death without receiving proper diagnosis and treatment, is not an instance in which I should simply count my blessing, but rather a moral failing and, in a loose sense, a crime against humanity.

With my international experience, my personal experience, as well as rounding out my education through IUP's Public Affairs program, I hope to achieve this goal of working and managing cholangiocarcinoma research and advocacy on a global scale. Not only will this degree allow me to reach new heights within these institutions, but I know firsthand the deep potential learning and growth on IUP's campus.

I hope that you will consider me for this program so that I can achieve these goals.

Christian was accepted to the IUP Graduate Studies program. I am eternally in awe of his courage, as expressed in these eloquently positive words. Nothing would stop him from being his authentic self, from taking leaps and bounds in changing the world, and from leaving an inspirational legacy for all to follow. He navigated his journey on its predestined course, remained calm, and shared his profound love with all in need. Throughout this book, as you've likely already noticed, it's been my aim to share tributes and anecdotes that are a testament to Christian's enormous presence in others' lives, whether they come from family, friends, or even people he only met in passing. No different religious or cultural viewpoint would prevent him from connecting with others. In fact, the curiosity to learn more from someone with a different outlook on life spurred on lasting connection.

Rose Camino wrote a few words, expressing the deep impact of Christian's character during their short interlude:

> What strikes me is what he represented. I didn't know him as long as the rest, but I could tell he enjoyed simple things. Family, friends, and experiences. I'm in awe of what he gave back in his short life and his everlasting impact on so many.
>
> I think it was well said, "You never know how one person's life impacts another," and he impacted mine: Your son was courageous and had the most beautiful smile. I think he was named right—Christian.

Michelle Luellen said the following:

> Most of us spend our entire lives trying to figure out our true purpose in this world. Christian Cochran had it sealed in his heart since birth. His purpose was to love, and he brought joy and love to everyone who knew him.
>
> His positivity was a gift from God. He looked for the good in each day. If he can do this while battling a rare and progressive form of cancer, I can certainly do this each day with minor aches and pains.

## Lessons Learned

Many people were touched by Christian's positive attitude and shared their personal experiences with our family. Here are a few testimonials we received after his passing that portray the life-changing effect of his gentle nature toward the people he interacted with:

Clay Vasey said,

> In the five years I've known Christian, he has brought much light to my life, whether he knew it or not. From the day I met him, he was easy to get along with and I enjoyed living with him, despite his slight aversion to cleaning!
>
> He tried to start a club that was formed exclusively to watch Seinfeld in the dormitory elevator. He called it "Seinfeld in the Elevator." He drew a decent crowd, but eventually the RAs shut it down.
>
> I remember the first time I had a girlfriend cheat on me during freshman year when I lived with Christian. When I found out, I slipped into a bit of a depression and Christian sensed that immediately without any prompting. I still remember vividly the hug he gave me. It didn't fix what happened, but it sure helped me get out of my "funk." Following that, he tried

extremely hard to cheer me up. He convinced me to go to parties and tried to set me up romantically with people he felt were compatible with me. I will forever appreciate the lengths he went to just see a smile on my face. He genuinely cared about my happiness and made it a priority.

In essence, he took the time to join me in doing things I enjoyed and did anything he could to put my bad days behind me, which made a world of difference to me.

Christian's maternal grandmother, Annie Bufalino, wrote a moving letter expressing her views of her beloved grandson, as follows:

I do not understand why some people have suffering in this life and why Christian suffered as he did. I only know that there was a higher purpose for his pain. God knew that Christian would accept this great suffering with great honor, just as he did.

One week before Christian died, my daughter Danielle called me and explained to me that Christian was receiving visits in his thoughts from an uncle of mine, who he never met or had occasion to hear us talk about. Christian didn't know of my uncle's existence at all.

Christian told his mother about these repeated visits, which occurred over several days, asking her who this person might be. He also confirmed a description of my uncle's physical appearance.

I feel that there was a deep spiritual connection being made here between my uncle and Christian. We can't know what meaning to place on a connection such as this, and as for the fact that the connection occurred at all, we can find no earthly explanation for.

However, we find this experience both remarkable and comforting.

Outside of this particular letter, Christian's grandmother also praises his loving kindness and accepting nature. She notes that he would always assume the role of peacemaker in situations of conflict. In particular, she shares how he would never judge others and how he enjoyed life's simple pleasures, remembering his calls of, "Grandma, Grandma, wake up, the sun is shining!" These virtues were lavishly shared with all. It occurred with his siblings, too: "It's okay Grandma, she's just being Kate," he'd say when he got picked on by his younger sister. Christian's grandmother also points out the relevance to Christian's character through his choice to become involved in his college's mock United Nations program, which he participated in throughout his college years.

His grandmother further recalled his love as a young boy, reading and spending many happy moments together with her. He always made her feel special and loved. She recalls how regularly Christian would call her from college to check in on her. He made her, just like everyone around him, feel the love that radiated abundantly from him.

There are also a couple of events that Danielle experienced, which we feel inclined to share. The first occurred when Christian was a young boy of approximately eight years. Christian, whose character was such that he rarely asked us for anything for himself, let alone on a repeated and pleading basis, tearfully implored Danielle all morning to promise him to plant a tree in his memory when he died.

Danielle, who was busily preparing for a get-together at our home, naturally found this request troubling, but did her best to assure Christian that there would be no need to memorialize him. Ultimately, simply to appease Christian—who would accept nothing less than her promise—Danielle gave him her word, not considering for a moment that such a circumstance would ever come to be.

Reflecting on young Christian's request, we find it especially poignant that cholangiocarcinoma is a disease of the bile duct, and the bile duct is sometimes referred to as the "biliary tree."

Danielle has always shown a gentle and loving way of interacting with the children. With that in mind, I think the second anecdote of hers— which I'll be sharing momentarily— reflects her profound motherly determination to help Christian, despite a situation that I'm compelled to believe may have been beyond her earthly capacity.

Let me preface Danielle's words by offering you some details for context: Christian had the habit of biting his fingernails from the time he was a young boy. He often tried to quit, but it never worked out for him. He bit them so much that the skin around them would bleed. As his parents, we were troubled by this. Was there something Christian was concerned about that we did not know? Did someone—perhaps even a heavenly being—approach him in some way and ask him to endure suffering? In the entry below, Danielle recalls the details following a discussion she had with Christian when he was in high school:

> I tried on several occasions to get Christian to stop biting his nails. The thing is that Christian had a very good life, with love and support from all his friends and family members. He really had nothing to be nervous about and no reason for such a habit. On one occasion, when I picked him up from high school, he got into the car and characteristically started biting his nails. I calmly touched his hand and drew it away from his mouth, and said in a soothing voice, "You don't need to bite your nails, sweetie." Christian replied, "Mom, you don't understand, I will always bite my nails and never stop." I proceeded to reassure him that everyone has their habits and encouraged him not to worry too much about it.
>
> I remember pausing to consider what to say next. Then—in a moment of clarity—I said to Christian that a time would come when he would know there would be no need to bite his fingernails any longer: it would be that simple. I was trying to reassure him to simply not worry about his habit. At the time, this experience with Christian seemed like an ordinary parental effort to guide and reassure a young adult child that everything would work out in time. When Christian was diagnosed with cancer, the memory of that exchange with Christian came back with harrowing clarity. I felt that Christian had much more to say than he did that afternoon when we had discussed his habit in the car.

Within days of his diagnosis, in another instance when Christian and I were alone, he said to me, "Mom, I don't need to bite my fingernails anymore because the worst thing I imagined could happen has just come true." From that moment on, Christian never bit his fingernails or skin around them again. He died with the most beautiful fingernails ever.

Now, we may all have our separate viewpoints on religion, faith, and spirituality. Some may want to prove everything scientifically, while others may take a philosophical approach. Some may not consider any connection between these events here at all. Others may approach and interpret these events esoterically.

As I'm sure you've learned by now, Christian certainly embraced a wide range of viewpoints and spiritual considerations. One thing that I can say for a fact, though, is that by no means would I, nor Christian, ever want to impose one specific viewpoint on spirituality—nor would we want to disrespect others' viewpoints. But through these events, the thread of a universal connection remains clear to me, and it's my belief that this thread stems from a celestial attempt to make us aware of a guiding light—and furthermore, a higher being. More precisely, a higher being with a plan.

Christian touched people's lives in a gentle, loving way. In doing so, he left them with a gift—one they did not even realize he gave them at that moment. Why? Because it was given in all humility. He didn't do things to be praised or recognized, he did them quietly and softly, knowing that he was doing the works of his Heavenly Father, with grace and humility.

One of the most enlightening handwritten notes we received after Christian's passing was from a school staff member who shared a story of how Christian saved another student's life. It reads as follows:

My treasured memory of Christian…

It was the Fall Play season and Chris and other cast and crew were in the auditorium daily into the evening. I was in the lobby visiting with students, and someone directed me to a message on the boys' bathroom wall. It was one of concern for another student. I remember asking the group (Christian among them) if they had seen anyone go into that restroom. Christian had, but before telling me, he walked in and read the message himself, wanting to see if he could help. As he walked toward me afterward, it was clear to see he knew something and was concerned.

He relayed to me the likely author of the message and who this person was concerned for. This concern resulted in a life being saved! The student was struggling and sad: Christian knew it, reported it, and was instrumental in allowing adults to intervene.

Christian was in the right place at the right time, kept a watchful eye on others, and saved the life of a friend of a friend. For those students on that day, Christian Cochran was what was good about today.

Next, here is a letter from Cassandra Lubic, one of Christian's treatment nurses at the UPMC Hillman Cancer Center at Passavant. She made a point of saying that during her eight years in oncology, "You care for so many people, but only a few will touch your heart and make an impact." For her, Christian was one of the few who impacted her life and will therefore stay in her heart. She knew that caring for him during treatment sessions would be challenging for her because of his tender age, but despite this, she started looking forward to their times together during chemotherapy. While she would assist and make him as comfortable as possible, he always brightened her days and made them better. They would talk endlessly about mutual interests, and in short, they developed a close friendship. Her words are as follows:

> Christian was a gift to every patient that came and sat in Pod 5 while he was receiving treatment. He would talk to anyone and everyone, regardless of who they were or how old they were. There were so many unique characteristics about him but the biggest one was how positive he remained throughout his journey with cancer. I have seen men in their 70s and 80s have the same diagnosis as this young man, and they would lash out,

throwing stuff across the room and being mad at the world. Christian not once made the pain he was experiencing visible.

In June 2021, Cassandra discovered that she was finally expecting a baby after she and her husband had tried to conceive for over a year. She never found the right opportunity to share the news with Christian due to his circumstances, but she knew that he would always be around and was aware of her great joy. She saw him in the changing color of the fall leaves (the season that Christian most loved) and his presence encouraged her to maintain the same happy outlook on life as she experienced while caring for him.

These excerpts—a few from a multitude of letters we have received—are a testament to the lessons that Christian's story brought to many people. Perhaps reading through them can help us to live more fulfilling lives, embrace gratitude for what we have, and become a little more compassionate and caring toward others.

# Embracing the Present

Christian lived in the moment. When he was in your presence, he was genuinely *there*. He cherished every connection, and every moment, and every day. This was his guiding example to us as a family and to the world at large. There are loads of personal stories from individuals from all walks of life who learned to embrace the present and find the beauty in small moments—all purely through Christian's influence.

A close group of four friends called themselves "The Clique" (Christian, Izzy, Bridget, and Megan), and though the nickname was pure fun, the bond that they shared was strong. Megan wrote to us that she will always cherish the special memories they created together. I'd like to now share some snippets from her letters to us:

> Performance was clearly one of Christian's many callings. Watching him on stage or during the marching band shows and student section, there was something so infectious about his energy and talent that kept your eyes glued to him.

> He truly changed the definition of love as I see it today. Christian taught me that love should always remain unconditional and it should favor the best parts of all of us. I saw that love in every single interaction I had with him and others. One important story that comes to mind occurred when we were visiting one of his favorite restaurants, Lulu's Noodles, in Oakland. As we were entering the restaurant, we were approached by a homeless man asking for money. I had quickly reacted to reject this man's pleas, but Christian immediately opened up his wallet, and without hesitation offered the man a $20 bill. After the interaction, I questioned why he would give that amount of money. He kindly reassured me that this man needed it, otherwise he wouldn't be asking. And if there was anything he could do to help, he wanted to do it. I think of this interaction, and Christian's saint-like level of generosity every time I see a homeless person and/or a person in need. He had the ability to see the best in every person, and treat them based on what he saw: something I try to emulate daily.
>
> His memory will always be what's good about today—every day.

Megan further shared an inspirational moment of calm comfort when she felt Christian's presence in the Basilica of the Shrine of the Immaculate during a visit. She experienced a "peaceful stillness" and felt "as if a weight had been lifted" from her chest. During that visit, she felt inspired to reconnect with her Saviour, and follow Christian's example of being a "true servant of God."

Another note that I'd like to share comes from Matt, who at the time was Kate's boyfriend, and as I write this is currently her fiancé. Matt was also a friend of Christian. Here is an excerpt from his letter:

> Christian oozed a charisma and character that any other high school aged kid could only dream of. He was the life behind PR's infamous drum-line every Friday night and always made their performance look comparable to a superbowl half-time production. By the time I began dating my middle school crush (Katie), I was more than familiar with Christian but was intimidated to talk to him, thanks to his larger-than-life

persona. Once I got to know Christian, though, I began to understand that he never thought of himself that way. He was always more interested in me and what I was doing, despite the fact that he was far more interesting in any way imaginable.

Visiting Christian and Katie at IUP are some memories I will truly never forget. There was the time that Katie had to do something for her sorority the night I came up to visit for the weekend. She would not be done for a number of hours and instead of sitting alone at her house, Christian suggested that we hang out while I waited. That night was the night that Christian truly became my big brother. Nothing earth-shattering or deep and insightful was said—more like four hours of cry-laughing at stupid YouTube videos, messing with his Japanese kendama toy, and making microwave mac and cheese—but it was genuinely Christian, and I will always cherish that memory. He made me feel special, like a big brother would to his younger brother.

I came to understand more and more that this genuine soul was just Christian, though—he was unapologetically himself in a way that I have never seen in even my closest friends. That is why he was special.

No one can understand the reasons behind anything that happened, but he never questioned it, and he stayed true to his faith with the same sense of humor and charisma through it all. Christian was the definition of strength and courage, and that is an enduring memory for me.

He was my greatest teacher over the past few years. Not just about how to have a sense of humor, or to not care what people think, or random history facts, or incredible thoughts about the wonders of space—but about how to treat others and ask for nothing in return and always remember what was good about today.

I do not feel like he is gone. In fact, I feel him watching over us every day while he's out there exploring the galaxy or making God laugh so much, his stomach hurts.

I take pride in the fact that these memories are mine to share and I had the chance to be a small part of a legacy that reaches even further than the stars.

[Letters shortened and adapted for readability.]

## Concluding Thoughts: Inspired by Christian

A role model teaches through life—through living a life with purpose without preaching. It means taking action against the wrongs and making a positive difference.

- Shape your world! Be the change. Your life has an impact. Make that impact visible.

- Affect change in meaningful ways. Hold on to optimism.

- Be authentically *you*. Become comfortable in your skin. Craft the legacy you want to leave behind.

- Find joy in simplicity. Find purpose in compassion. Offer help without questioning.

- Accept your journey.

- Make peace. *Be* the peacemaker.

# Chapter 5:

# A Father's View

I'd like to share an anecdote reflecting Christian's gentle compassion for all living things. On one of our wedding anniversaries, Danielle requested lobster, and when I came home with the live crustacean in hand, Christian was curious to see it. He thought it was the coolest creature and he even named it—Bob. He didn't know that it was meant for dinner! When he discovered the fate of the poor lobster, he begged us—crying—not to cook and eat poor Bob. Needless to say, with such strong opposition, Bob's life was saved.

This was Christian at a young age, but he maintained this compassionate characteristic throughout his entire life. The following is a poem contributed by Christian's aunt and uncle—Bridgie and Davey, as he called them—who were very close to him.

>For Christian

>Who learned, and by example, shared

>what he seemed always to know.

>First wave to the gut,

>Creatures of the sea,

>Aversion to anything dying

>Dignity of the deep.

>Soon, the stars and planets

And always, everything connected,

To the land—

Adventures with adored everyone,

Hiking,

Camping,

Beach,

Bikes and Kites,

Trees too—

Noble, brave, rooted with unbound tops,

Curling brilliantly with the wind.

Love forever, Bridgie and Davey

## My Paternal Observations

Christian was always grateful for life and all that was in it. He never took anything for granted and never wavered from the opportunity to make someone's day special and make them feel loved. He truly understood our purpose here on Earth—to unconditionally love and help one another. He did this better than anyone I have ever met in my lifetime. Perhaps that is why he only had that one regret in his life: doing too much homework!

Christian understood that he was not in control of where his cancer would take him. He understood that he was merely in control of his *response* to it, and that response was to enjoy the time that he had left with the people, pets, and activities he loved the most. He spent his entire life being mindful of the *quality* of life and he achieved this even after his diagnosis. He couldn't change his situation—only his attitude of making the best of it.

This mindful approach to life was something that he chose to lead as a matter of keen interest. He was captivated by Taoism and its teachings. He shared some of his interests in Taoism with his mother and enjoyed reading *The Tao of Pooh* by Benjamin Hoff (1982). When he became ill, his mindset was in line with the Taoist way of thinking. The philosophy was ingrained in his being and became a useful tool when diagnosed. Danielle wrote in the *CaringBridge* journal once: "Certainly this year has produced some 'vinegar' in our lives, but Christian has taught me a lot, and he has shown me that bitterness and sourness can cause interference with appreciativeness and gratitude. So, we will continue to smile when we taste 'vinegar,' knowing that we are on a journey of healing, learning, and growing."

In Taoist philosophy, the interfering and unappreciative mind leaves the person discontented whereas the sweetness of life comes from an understanding and acceptance that life is what it is. This message is clear from *The Vinegar Tasters* in Hoff's book, which Christian loved so much. Hoff wrote the book in the evenings and over weekends while being a tree pruner by trade in the Portland Japanese Garden at Washington Park, Portland. He allegorically used A. A. Milne's *Winnie the Pooh* characters to express the Taoist belief system to Western society and explain its basic principles.

The book is eloquently introduced with a description of the famous 16th-century Eastern painting of the *Vinegar Tasters*—three great Eastern thinkers presenting Confucianism, Buddhism, and Taoism as they are tasting vinegar from a vat (Wikipedia, 2022, para 2):

> The three men are Confucius, Buddha, and Laozi, respectively. Each man's expression represents the predominant attitude of his philosophy: Confucianism saw life as sour, in need of rules to correct the degeneration of people; Buddhism saw life as

bitter, dominated by pain and suffering due to the attachment of possessions and material desires; and Taoism saw life as sweet, due to it being fundamentally perfect in its natural state. Another interpretation of the painting is that, since the three men are gathered around one vat of vinegar, the "three teachings" are one.

The vinegar represents life, and while Confucius finds it sour and Buddha finds it bitter, Lao Tzu finds it satisfying. From this life metaphor, Hoff unfolds the rest of the Taoist philosophy. He accentuates the Taoist concept of "effortless doing" and an unsophisticated problem-solving worldview as it is represented by Winnie the Pooh—as opposed to Owl and Rabbit who complicate things and Eeyore who pessimistically frets about life instead of just being. At the core of Taoism is the concept that the Tao gives birth to all of life—in fact, it's the driving force behind all of life—and thus it is everything even in its invisible state. Therefore, every natural thing remains good when it remains true to its nature and when it's not being judged, named, or forcefully altered. It simply *is*, and when a person acknowledges that life simply is as it is represented in its natural and harmonious state, the experience remains good.

The book is an analogy to human nature and it influenced Christian greatly. He was in line with the thoughts of Lao Tzu and the smile on his face: a sweet expression after tasting the vinegar and merely experiencing the taste without judgment. From the perspective of "this is only vinegar," the taste doesn't have to be anything at all—it is only itself. And in this way, Taoism—and Christian—acknowledged and participated in the harmonious predestined flow of nature and life itself. Christian never imposed his way, he followed "*the* way." Whatever the taste of life, it was perfect in its natural state.

At times, his friends would ask him for a ride, and he wouldn't hesitate to take them home—even if he had to drive long distances. He would never ask for anything in return. Occasionally, he would come home much later and when Danielle asked him where he was, he would reply that so-and-so needed a ride home. Christian had many virtues and was notably a wonderful friend to many people. I love how Jay Carson (Emeritus Professor of English Studies at Robert Morris University) captures a sense of Christian as an unconditional loving friend. It resulted in the following beautiful poem:

Christian

He was not my son

or even my nephew or distant cousin

but I loved him in the way

of the older admiring charming youth:

from grace of movement

to curly crown to Joel McCrea

Hollywood handsome face.

Even in all that light

it was his ease of movement

among men and women

that grabbed us.

The yearning that we all had

to be in his glowing space,

a turn of phrase or joke

that made me feel I had never so well

understood the full magic of language.

There was no gimme back in his nature,

but a skipping generosity to all.

For the young friends needing rides

to older neighbors needing kindly words.


National flags were one of his passions

showing a curiosity for the world

and an acceptance of the beauty of all.


And Christian was a fine actor

starring and entertaining his classmates, family,

playing his way into our hearts.

I love how the poem summarizes Christian's playful way of climbing into our hearts. I know that he still lives in many hearts, and always will.

## Christian and Rachael

The first time I heard about the night Christian met his girlfriend, it felt as though I was there in Prague with them, witnessing the beginning of their remarkable journey. It was on September 1st, 2018—just three days into Rachael's adventure in the city, that fate decided to bring these two young adults together. My son, known for his ability to light up any room with his laughter and impromptu dance moves, met someone who would hold a special place in his life.

Rachael recalled their initial encounter with such clarity and warmth that I could almost see Christian through her eyes: "The first night we met, I thought he was shy, but he quickly gave way to the outgoing and endearing personality we all recognize in him," she said to me. Despite being surrounded by new faces and the excitement of being abroad, there was an instant connection between them. At their newly occupied apartment, Christian made everyone comfortable with his quick wit of jokes and quirky dance moves, helping to forge a newly formed group of friends that would stay close as the semester unfolded and beyond. A spark ignited in the heart of Prague that first night of their meeting—holding the promise of something unforgettable.

Their friendship developed swiftly, grounded in shared experiences and countless moments that brought them closer. From their laughter-filled dinners to dancing the night away, their connection deepened with each shared adventure: At Lucerna Music Bar, his dance moves became the highlight of their evenings. Hearing about their escapades, from photography class outings to Harry Potter binge-watching weekends, their adventures painted a vivid picture of two people perfectly in sync.

Christian's willingness to be there for her, even on difficult days after challenging tests, spoke volumes about his character. His supportive nature and his ability to make the best out of every situation were qualities that resonated deeply with her. As Christian's father, learning about their journey—from the hesitant beginnings of their relationship to the defining moments that cemented their bond—filled me with a sense of pride and joy. Their story unfolded like a film, with its ups and downs, laughter, and heartfelt conversations culminating in a love that was both profound and uplifting.

Their adventures didn't stop in Prague. From introducing Christian to her family and friends (who were quickly won over by his charm and genuine interest in getting to know them) to planning their future together filled with dreams of a family (they even selected names for their children: Lily or Oscar), homes (an A-frame in particular), and careers—their story was a testament to the power of connection and shared dreams. Rachael described the impact that Christian had on her life in the following journal entry:

> Christian was the kindest, most thoughtful, funniest person I had ever met. He was like a breath of fresh air—the boyfriend of boyfriends, always carrying his natural, caring, funny, loving

gifts with him. He was truly the most interesting person ever with his vast knowledge and understanding of the world. I admired that he was completely comfortable expressing his feelings. He was a ball of sunshine ready to take on the world and brighten it for all.

Christian was my biggest supporter with school, extracurriculars, and everything else going on. He would always tell me how proud he was of me and encouraged me to keep going. This meant so much. He told people what he felt and inspired you to build you up. He understood the power of loving and supporting the people in your life. He was comfortable listening to me when I had to vent and let it all out and be negative for a while. No matter what I needed (or anyone else, for that matter), he was there: unconditionally and nonjudgmentally.

He was the one who made me believe I could go to law school and be a lawyer. At one point, I really wanted to be a judge, and he surprised me with a gavel he found in an antique shop in Pittsburgh. That gavel is on my desk in my Philadelphia law office to this day, and if I ever become a judge, that's the one I'm using.

Christian and Rachael's love story is one of love and laughter—a reminder to cherish the people in our lives and to love fully, no matter what. He showed us the importance of being present, caring deeply for others, and facing life with a positive spirit.

# From Helplessness to Light

It's impossible to find the words to express the range of emotions that I experienced while watching a son battle cancer. I don't wish this on anyone. There were times when I was so distraught that even I couldn't comprehend the manifestations of my grief. What made it even more difficult was having to watch my beautiful wife and other children suffer the same way. The fact that we are such a close-knit family can be a great thing, as we are highly supportive of each other, but it can also be an extremely painful thing to behold during the grieving process. The pain I had to endure while watching my family suffer was an additional strain.

I won't lie: There were tough days when I couldn't hold it together. But what really held me through it all was the courage and compassion that I found in observing Christian's situation. My gentle son was a phenomenal inspiration to me—and to all of us. It sparked energy in me, steering me on a journey of helping him to find a cure and some relief for his suffering. It didn't end there: Christian's trust in his loved ones set an unforgettable example for me. His unconditional support for others directed my quest to take action and not fall back into the darkness of despair.

About four months after Christian's diagnosis, I started making notes on my notepad. This journaling method helped me to jot down my overwhelming feelings wherever I went. Many of my worst thoughts and fears arrived in the ghostly hours after midnight when I was lying in bed—wide awake and listening to the sleeping world. My emotions have ranged from fear and helplessness, back to hope, and then back to hopelessness again. It felt like a roller-coaster ride, and every new day brought new emotions while I watched my beautiful son battle this cancer. My grief manifested in every way one could imagine. At the beginning of the new year, I wrote the following in my journal:

> January, 2021
>
> The day started off like most days: feeling down and really low. Both Danielle and I feel like crawling under a rock most of the time. The weight of Christian's cancer has felt crushing at times. We are both tired and we do not want to talk to anyone.
>
> Nick and I went to go look for a Playstation 5. Even though we couldn't find one, I was happy to do something with him.
>
> We're all on pins and needles for Christian's upcoming CT and PET scans. The last two days have been filled with tremendous stress, and the burden of it all has seemed to catch up with Christian.

I am so scared of losing Christian. The joy he gives us is like a breath of air to us—to me.

When I cry at night, I think about the dark places where my mind wanders. I think about Danielle, Kate, and Nicholas. How do I keep this family together? It's hard enough keeping it together now, what will happen when we lose Christian? What will that do to us as a family? We are so close.

I really don't want to speak to people. Talking to friends is so difficult because no one really understands the trajectory of our emotional pain. They try, they pray, and they tell us that they support us—but how could they truly know how we suffer?

Today, we had to be at the hospital at 6 a.m. Waking up was easy, but going to my son's room to wake him for yet another test was emotional. Danielle was crying in the bedroom and I had to stay strong and treat the morning like any other. Like, "Hey, no big deal, we're just going in to do a scan that will tell us if my son will make it or not." My emotions are indescribable, profoundly deep, and never-ending.

I don't say this lightly, but I believe that Christian is a living modern day saint walking among us mere mortals. It goes beyond strength to mightiness: possessing a dignified power.

I want him to know before I leave this Earth (hopefully well before him...) how much I love him, how much I care for him, and how much he means to me. I hope he knows how much he means to everyone on this earthly planet.

Well, it's the day after the scans and we are all just going about our business as usual. Yet, looming in the background, we are all desperately and quietly awaiting the results. Christian is having a great day. That makes it easier for us. It's still so tough to watch him, though...

Today is a pretty day. It's Saturday, the sun is out, and the weather is great: perfect football weather. I'm watching football while Christian is on his computer with his friends having a great time. It's profoundly challenging to know that my son is just in the next room, dealing with his illness. Today he mentioned that he's thinking about buying an antique replica rifle to display over his fireplace once he has his own place. He seems to think it would be a cool decoration.

I love hearing him make plans for the future. It might seem odd, but just having normal conversations about everyday things, even something like buying an antique replica gun, makes me happy. This might be hard for others to understand, but it's very meaningful to me.

My thoughts venture to dreams. As a father, prior to Christian's diagnosis, I used to dream about stuff like vacations, money, children's futures, decorating, cars, helping others, or being a professional athlete. The list is long. Now, I don't dream anymore, except about Christian's health. Thoughts about Christian's health are my last ones of the day before I try to sleep, and my first ones when I wake: every single day!

It's Sunday. The Lord tells us not to fear. My fear is so real and constant. My fear is that Christian will not be here this time next year.

Christian also has emotions that run between highs and lows, and I know that he wants to live—this I know for sure: He talks about his love of life and wanting to live.

My mind is very weak. My emotions change by the minute. Most days, I struggle to focus. I try to hide my pain from others. Some days I take pills to help, other days, I just try to fall asleep as quickly as possible. Living is hard work. I love my family so much and I would never leave them. To be honest, sometimes they are the only reason why I want to live. Without them, I'll be lost and empty. Losing Christian would put me in a place I hope I never have to meet.

When I hear Christian talk to Danielle, it makes me feel so happy and joyful. It pierces my body like an arrowhead and I feel it in my heart.

During this time, we had a strange experience connected to dreaming. Nicholas had a call from Gregg Broujos, a family friend. As part of a school project, Nicholas, Christian's younger brother, had to interview a real estate professional. At the end of the call, Gregg told Nick, "Give your brother a big hug for me." Christian was away at the time, spending time with Rachael.

The next day, Christian sent me a text message about having a strange dream the night before. He said, "I had a dream, don't remember much of it, but Nick gave me a big hug in it. Made me really happy." Now, the strange part is that Christian usually didn't share his dreams, nor did he mention Nick hugging him in general. (Anyone who knows Nicholas will know that he is not a "hugger.") To make it even more mysterious, Nick told us that he intended to hug Christian on his return.

I know that God works in mysterious ways, but my mind was blown away. I clearly saw this as another example of a higher being trying to tell us something. I spent the rest of that day pacing my thoughts and questions in my head, trying to figure out what the dream could mean. I wrote the following:

> Christian arrived with Rachael after their time together, feeling elated. They had a great time. I'm so proud of my son. Every day, I feel closer to him. We explore so much together, share such deep thoughts and passions. He is so smart. He is like the greatest book with many compelling chapters.
>
> Watching Christian's struggle is taking a toll on me and Danielle. It's so difficult to watch your beautiful son—whose life held such promise—hurt so much. Now, his path is filled with challenges and hardships. I still believe he is a fighter.
>
> Thank God I have Danielle in my life. This process is so taxing on us, not only mentally but also physically. We need solutions and actions!

After we had some discussions about his anticipated TIL trial, we felt a little more positive. We had a thread of hope to follow again. Still, the day of the discussions about the trial created its own emotional journey with the whole family. I turned to my journal to verbalize my emotions and tried to make sense of the situation by writing this:

> When we got home, he went straight to the basement to make his online calls for ADP to sell HR and Payroll services. Can you imagine anything more ridiculous than this?? I mean: Really? He is selling nonessentials on a phone to strangers who hang up on him or are mean to him!
>
> I told him to seriously consider putting these things on hold now and focus on his health.
>
> I tell him to remember to take everything "day by day" and focus on today, not tomorrow. Forget about yesterday, because you cannot change that. I can see he tries to embrace this but it must be so hard for him.

For a few months after January, I didn't write down my thoughts. Not that they weren't nagging at me, but we just became increasingly busy and occupied with taking things day by day and focusing on Christian's health. We were getting ready for the TIL trial and had to deal with the stress of weeks without chemotherapy while his fragile body suffered. My last words in a journal entry in March 2021 were, "Christian is so destined to be successful at changing the world."

I didn't write again until after Christian's passing. And then my mourning ventured into the darkest moments of my entire life. My thoughts rushed between anger, despair, and a deep depression like I had never before encountered. At the end of November 2021, my journal notes were laced with perpetual sadness:

> There is really little good in this life.
>
> Danielle, Kate, and Nick are all that matters.
>
> I wish I was a better man and could keep it together.
>
> I really don't care about tomorrow.
>
> I'm seeking meaning for this life. What's the purpose of taking my son away from me?

I'm so tired all the time.

I don't like when people tell me I "created" Christian. I did not create him. He created himself. I wish I could say I had something to do with it, but I didn't. He was always better than me.

I realize now that it was me learning from Christian.

How will my story end? Can I live up to what's in front of me?

In December of that year, I felt more and more exposed and vulnerable when I ventured into public spaces. I felt naked when I sat somewhere and saw people "knowingly" looking at me. It felt like there was a perpetual barrier between my world and theirs: as if I was standing on the outside of something that I remembered so well but couldn't access anymore. I desperately wanted to be myself again. I wanted to go back to the life I knew before Christian's passing, but I couldn't remember it clearly. I struggled to relate to other people, as I sensed that I understood something they tried to understand, but couldn't. I felt like a foreigner in a distant land.

I couldn't imagine them knowing the torture inflicted on my soul with the loss of my elder son. I dreaded the approaching festive season, filled with so many beautiful memories from yesteryear. Living without Christian was dark and bland. Anger would well up in me and inside my skull. I would swear and curse the universe and everything that robbed me of my former joyfulness. Even though I knew that it was what Christian would have wanted, I failed to achieve it as I pined for his presence. I felt increasing despair.

The only thing that kept me on this Earth was the thought of my beautiful wife and my incredible children. I held on to them like a boat needing an anchor to steady its course in the wind. "Sorry Christian, I wish I could be more like you," I wrote just before Christmas 2021.

In April, of the next year, my last journal note was this:

> Well, it's been a while since I have written anything, but I suspect it's been my sheer lack of mental effort. Today is beautiful.

In hindsight: What a profound note! *What's good about today?* Today is beautiful, I wrote... Every day is a new day, further away from the pain of that loss. I know it won't go away. But I'm learning to hold my son differently. I'm learning to follow him. Christian's ability to never judge was his most beautiful gift to us. I keep asking him to help me do the same. I ask him for strength. I ask him to get me through each day. I know that I have the most incredible family and I have to improve myself to be the best for them. I ask God and Christian all the time to help me with this. I ask them to give me the strength to move forward.

We all mourn loss differently. My way is different from my wife's way, and different from Christian's sister, Kate, and his brother, Nicholas. There is no right or wrong way. And it's painful, whichever way the mourning shakes our roots. I see my family suffer through this long and ever-present process, and I feel for them. I want to take it all away from them. But—I have also found an unbreakable bond in sharing the loss of our beloved son and brother. That bond requires no words.

# Appreciating Small Things

Christian prevented me from falling into despair by helping me to find the beautiful and the positive in every moment, every day. There are specific moments that stand out more than others, and they all affected our journey and our attitude to the new future we were facing as a family.

After Christian's passing, we were faced not only with overwhelming emotions but with a deep desire to reconnect and be assured of Christian's happiness. I distinctly remember (approximately two to three weeks before he passed away) kneeling next to his bed in the living room and burying my head into Christian's neck while he was lying down. I remember trying my best to wish his illness away and thinking to myself that what was happening wasn't real. I kissed his neck and told him how much I loved him. He told me that he loved me *more*. (He often used this expression of love: loving someone more than they love him.) I used to keep my tears away from Christian, even though I wanted to cry with him often. He managed to muster enough strength to reach his right arm over and calmly put it on my head saying, "Everything is going to be okay, Dad."

We kept a picture of Christ on our fireplace mantle which pointed toward Christian's bed in our living room. He looked up at the picture and said, "I really love that guy" in his weakened voice. Then he asked me, "Who do you think I will see first when I get to heaven, Dad?" I said, "Christian, I'm confident that Christ himself will be the first to greet you there. You are important to him." During this conversation, I also said, "I need you to make a promise to me, Christian." He responded, "Of course, Dad, anything." I told him, "I need you to come and visit me after you arrive in heaven. I know you will be busy and I am sure everyone will want your attention, but I need you to come see me to let me know you're okay." He promised me that he would do this.

I'd like to share some of the following visions and encounters with you and I firmly believe they were not mere imaginations. Too many things indicated the opposite. Christian died on September 1st, 2021. This was a Wednesday. On Friday, that same week, I walked down my driveway to my mailbox. I could hear the mail truck coming down the street so I thought I would just greet the mailwoman. She was a very kind person who had heard of Christian's passing. I waited at the mailbox until she pulled up. Something extraordinary happened.

As the mailwoman reached out to hand me our mail, a beautiful butterfly came from nowhere and landed on my hand that was reaching to take the mail from her. The large butterfly was bright blue—a color that I had never seen before in my entire life. We rarely see butterflies in our neighborhood, except for a few small ones on rare occasions. But I have certainly not seen such a large one, let alone such a bright blue one, and even less one that landed as our hands met. It stayed on my hand for a good 10 seconds while the mailwoman and I exchanged surprised looks in absolute silence and shock. The only thing I said to her was, "Are you seeing what I am seeing or am I imagining this right now?" She said, "No, you are seeing what I'm seeing." Then the butterfly fluttered into the air and disappeared as if it had never been there at all.

We were both stunned and silent. She confirmed my thoughts by saying that the occurrence was beyond this world, and then told me, "You know, your son is so special because he would always go out of his way to say hello to me and ask me how I'm doing. If he passed me in the car, he would stop to say hello and tell me to have a wonderful day. Sometimes, he would only wave, but he would always acknowledge me. No one else does that to me." She told me that people generally ignore her or just walk the other way when she shows up. But Christian would always go out of his way to check in on her. She had a challenging life, yet Christian somehow knew he had to make her feel welcome. He didn't have to do so, but he did anyway because he knew how important a sincere connection was to her. Reflecting on this incident conjures up profound thoughts of how Christian sensed her sadness and gave her all the more love and kindness that she didn't find elsewhere.

A week later, I had another otherworldly experience while waking up just after 3 a.m. I was lying in bed with my wife. It all started with me being transported to the basement of a house. I was very confused. It seemed like it was newly constructed; the basement was empty with cinderblock walls and a concrete floor. I stood there looking at a sliding door and remember saying to myself, "I need to get out of here because I'm in the wrong place." After this thought, I was transported to a foyer with a squared ceramic floor. I stood at the wooden front door: It had three vertical, narrow window slots. Again, I thought I was in the wrong house but somehow the door was familiar to me. It looked like a 1970s door. I stared at it for a few moments, then turned left to look into the main room. I remember feeling a warm light all around me.

The place was decorated in yellow patterns and there were two large yellow chairs in front of me. They were positioned facing each other. In the distance, I could see the kitchen, which was a step up from the living room. There was activity in the kitchen and also people sitting in the chairs. But the people were all shadow figures. While the people in the kitchen—about four or five of them—were moving around, the shadow figures in the chairs swiveled around to look at me. I thought to myself that I must be at a dinner party or something. To the left was a large fireplace with a crackling fire.

It was then that I saw Christian standing at the fireplace with his curly hair and hand on the mantle—giving me the biggest smile, as if to say, "See, I promised." He was dressed casually in a sweater. We locked eyes, and in my excitement of seeing him smile, I said, "Christian," and started moving toward him. In that instant, before I could move, his face came up to a few inches away from mine. We hugged deeply. I could feel all of him! It was as real as any hug I had had with him on earthly terms. I could even smell Christian's distinct scent.

The most incredible part was that he started talking but without his lips moving. I could hear him speak to me, and the first exchanges were about how much we love each other. He then told me, "Dad, please tell Mom that I love her." He continued in a stern voice, "You and Mom need to know that I'm okay. I want you both to move on."

After that, it felt as if I slowly glided back into my body. I opened my eyes. I lay in bed, staring at the ceiling trying to understand what took place in front of my eyes. I was overwhelmingly aware of the profound connection that had just happened. I didn't want to wake Danielle as I lay there digesting what had just happened. I decided to tell her about Christian's visit in the morning. At that moment, she asked me if I was awake because she heard something. I was still motionless after the experience, but wide awake.

I relayed my experience to her right there because I knew I had just returned from something very important. (She recorded the conversation, not that I would ever forget it!) She asked me if it felt like a dream and I told her no—not at all. It felt like a reality, "As real as I am here talking with you," I said to Danielle. I know, without a shadow of a doubt, that I was invited to a rare encounter with another world. Christian and I met in a special place, after special permission, for a moment in time. Unbeknownst to me at the time, Danielle explained that she had been praying very deeply before we fell asleep, asking Christian to show her a sign that he was okay. It was clear to both of us that Christian lived up to his promise to me and listened to his mother.

Earlier that evening, Danielle was extremely upset and standing on our back deck looking up at the moon and stars while talking to God and Christian. (Danielle related this experience to me the next morning.) In her anguished tears, she was crying to them to let her know that he was safe and doing alright. Her words were mostly directed at Christian, as if he were in front of her, in a worrisome but loving way of a concerned mother. She shared her fears with him: She was now physically separated from him and was very concerned about her firstborn child. In her anguish, she firmly told them that Christian must let her know that he was safe.

Although I have asked Christian—selfishly—to come and visit me, he has shown himself in so many ways to us and also to others. Five months after he passed away, Danielle and I decided to get out of town for a break. We were in dire need of an escape from what was familiar, but so very broken. I booked a flight for us to go to Florida, to be in warmer weather that might soothe our hurt a little. When we boarded the plane, a good friend of mine, Dave, and his girlfriend, Melissa, were also there. I still do not know if it happened by coincidence or whether fate had a role to play.

We hadn't met his girlfriend before. She was well aware of our family's situation, familiar with Christian's story, and proved to be a kind, sweet person. Dave was always highly supportive of my family during difficult times. Danielle and I were both surprised to see him. We passed them on the plane, said hello, and took our seats further back. We didn't think much more of it until he sent me a text while we were taxiing to the runway, inviting us back down to Florida a few months later.

Danielle and I were not really sure what to do with this invitation because we didn't feel very sociable during that period of mourning. We simply wanted to remain isolated and distant from anyone who knew us. Somehow, despite these overwhelming thoughts, we still said, "Sure." Unlike us, we didn't say "We'll see" or "Maybe" or something like that. Instead, we simply looked at each other and without a doubt accepted the invitation: as if something was telling us that we must go. And so we did. We relayed messages and I booked a flight right there on the plane for the upcoming visit.

A few months later, we went to Naples, Florida with Dave and Melissa. Danielle felt comfortable with her since there were no memories of raising children together, as with other couples. She was someone new in our lives, and it was less painful for us to be around new people. On our first night there after dinner, she went to bed before us. The three of us (Dave, Danielle, and I) stayed on the porch, telling stories and laughing together. The following occurred—I relay his girlfriend's remarkable experience in her words directly, as she later wrote them down for me:

> We invited Danielle and Christopher Cochran to our home in Naples, Florida. I met them about a month ago when we ran into each other at the airport. I told my partner that we should invite them to Florida soon, and we did.
>
> On Thursday, April 21st, 2022, we had a great day and a late night together. When I went to bed, this occurred:
>
> I know Christian wanted you to know that he is always watching you and had a message for me to give to you. I don't know him and never met him, but that night, a blurry shadow of him appeared. We had spent a fun day with you and Danielle together as friends.
>
> All I could see was his dark hair, but he spoke to me and said, "I really want to thank you for inviting my parents and bringing them here with you. Thank you for having fun with them. They need to start living life again. And I really want to see a smile on my mom's face again."

In her notes, she further wrote:

> Christian's Heavenly Spirit—talking to me: I could feel it was important to him. He was genuine. I wasn't sure how to tell you and Danielle or whether it would upset you so I didn't say anything the next morning. While we were sitting at the pool, Danielle was talking about him and got emotional. I could feel him nudge me twice to tell you what he said to me. ("Tell her, you can tell her what I said to you," Christian nudged.)

> He didn't want to see you sad.
>
> I asked Dave if I should tell you, since I didn't want to upset you both. He said I should absolutely share the experience with you. I've not had such an experience before. I'm not sure why Christian went through me to you, but I feel honored. It was good to tell you about this experience at the pool.
>
> From your stories about him, Christian sounds like an angel with a beautiful soul. He inspires me to be a better person. You both raised an amazing young man with a heart and soul of pure gold. He was meant for so much more on this Earth. From what you've told me—and more so after my close experience with him.

She told us that she was never afraid while in Christian's presence: She felt a remarkable peace. The words that she shared with us were very similar to what Christian would have said. Christian encouraged her to relay the message from him to us. It's truly remarkable.

It's not fully understood what grief does to the body, but it has been found that early after loss, people do experience encounters of seeing or feeling the departed. These bereavement encounters during a heightened state of emotional turmoil are not delusions or psychoses. They are completely harmless—in fact, they can be comforting during the painful process of mourning, as they make the bereaved person feel that their departed loved one is still around. They also aid the separation process and assist in healing. Creating, reliving, or experiencing moments with the loved one certainly serves a purpose. Catching a glimpse of a deceased loved one or a scent triggering a thought are actually healthy ways of coping with the emotional pain.

I do believe that our encounters with Christian were real and they were coming from a place of his deep concern about his family. He *wanted* to present himself to us and assure us of his well-being. His empathetic nature made him highly intuitive to the emotions of others and he strived to soothe us all, both before and after his passing.

# Thoughts: Inspired by Christian

As a father, I have been a student of my son's guidance. I have learned to accept the course of our journey as a family, despite the trails of hardship.

- Don't take things for granted.

- Follow your intuition.

- You can't control the course. You can only control your response to it. Make the best of every situation. Nature remains good in its unforced and unjudged state. Simply be.

- Discontentment and interference ruin understanding and acceptance.

- Offer unconditional support. Share your loss: You are not alone.

- Share your feelings. Say you love someone. Hug them.

Chapter 6:

# 8,508 Days

*Therefore the sage manages affairs without doing anything, and conveys his instructions without the use of speech.* –Lao Tzu

Christian's life was a journey of love. Every day of his journey was spent in the presence of compassion, kindness, and enthusiasm. He was able to live a life of purpose and his example inspired all of us. Each one of his 8,508 days on this Earth was lived intentionally.

## Christian's 8,508-Day Life Path

Living a purposeful life is living a life with positive intentions. It means taking each day for what it offers, finding the joy and contentment within that, and sharing connections with others in a lovingly meaningful way that enables confidence and trust. A life of gratitude can be cultivated with practical steps to feed your intentions. Many studies have pointed out the benefits of keeping gratitude journals, engaging in random acts of kindness to strangers or loved ones, conducting sincere self-care, writing a self-compassion letter, training your thoughts to shift attention to the positive, practicing emotional regulation strategies to downplay negativity, or trying out mindfulness and positivity meditations.

We all have strengths, just as we all have our weaknesses. It's perfectly normal. That's what makes us human. Any imbalance in this—either to being overly negative or being overly positive—defies our true essence. However, shifting from a negative state of mind to an intentionally positive state of mind reframes our concept of life as we hack our brains to believe what we want them to believe. The crucial element to doing this is to be authentic: Fake positivity has no meaningful intention.

In addition to this, living a meaningful and mindful life—daily—redefines our nature. Christian knew this. He was intuitively aware of his predestined path and he didn't resist its course. Instead, he focused on each moment and he made the best of it. We observed him doing that as we counted the days with him. His journey became one of living purposefully, in the here and now—every single day.

Now, I would like to pass the narrative over to Danielle once more, to share more on this aspect of Christian's life.

## *A Mother's* Impressions

It has been the privilege of a lifetime to be the mother of Christian Anthony Cochran. For 23 years, I have been blessed to call him my son. Before I ever met him, I knew he would be named Christian. I did not have any other names planned for him. Christian was always meant to be Christian—a servant of Christ.

I was always so proud of him: the way he carried himself with love, humility, and grace. He was smart beyond his years—intellectually, emotionally, and spiritually. Notably so, even from early youth. He made me proud to be in his presence and take him places. As a young child, people would approach him, coming up to his beaming face with his trademark curly hair. Somehow, even beyond his cherubic physical appearance, he would always draw people over, spread his joy, and find ways to make them smile. He had a natural way; a knack for making people feel better about their days and about themselves. You could just see it. He always had something kind to say to others—and he was just as kind to them when they were not even present.

Much of the time when in public, Christian would greet others. He would frequently say *hello* and beam his warm smile at passersby. He would then often bestow a compliment of some sort—something you probably wouldn't have noticed yourself, until Christian spoke up. Invariably, you'd recognize the genuine aptness of his compliment—you might even break into a big smile. These brief and beautiful exchanges often occurred in stores with cashiers and with waitstaff in restaurants. He always wanted to ignite a joyful feeling and spread love everywhere he went. It was wonderful to observe his effect on others: his natural ability to make people smile, laugh, and feel good.

Christian always wanted to be a light in the darkness and would often demonstrate, by example, not to judge people. "You never know what someone could be going through," he would say. Even though he was always this way, he became more determined to spread his light during his final year in the midst of—and in response to—his illness. He noticed the person who was hurting, or alone, or the one who needed help. He was a keen and sympathetic observer. Even at a very young age, Christian had the compassion and confidence to reach out to those in need. He cultivated peace wherever he went.

From the get-go, my beautiful son was very verbal. I recall, at his nine-month doctor's appointment, him sharing all the words he knew to the doctor who was visibly impressed and even observed that it was "highly unusual." Christian was able to say his "Our Father" and "Hail Mary" completely before the age of three. He also showed a profound curiosity, inclusiveness, and love from a young age toward various cultures and people from around the world. He talked to me about possibly joining the Peace Corps and planned to go to graduate school to study Public Policy so he could help adults and children in underprivileged countries obtain medical care—especially those suffering from rare cancers. He wanted to make a meaningful impact on people without access to good medical treatment. After his cancer diagnosis, he considered himself fortunate to have access to highly trained specialists and developed experimental medications, and he wanted to do his part in helping the less fortunate gain similar access to these as well. He was so grateful to all of his doctors and nurses for everything they did for him and expressed his gratitude to all of them on every occasion they met.

As his parents, witnessing our son's struggle with an incurable illness created many instances of disillusionment with his treatment regimens and the medical system throughout his care. Yet, Christian himself remained staunch and unwavering in his gratitude and respect for all of his caregivers.

Christian's love was universal. It crossed all boundaries: cultural, ethnic, racial, and religious. He had so many friends. He never judged. He only shared his bright light and showed his deep love to everyone. He wasn't afraid of being unique. He was full of passion for everything he set out to do in life and could notice suffering from a mile away. When he did, he'd make sure that he touched that person with his empathy, love, and kindness. He would smile, start up a conversation, and seek ways to help that person in any way he could. He was confident in who he was.

Christian shared his love of Christ and spiritual beliefs unobtrusively with all. He would listen to others, open up a dialogue, and then quietly plant seeds about kindness and spirituality. His faith embraced all religions respectfully and he engaged in a nonjudgmental spiritual way with all.

Christian adored us—his family. He also showed tremendous respect for us and was committed to bringing us pride and happiness. Even through his teenage years, when most teenagers awkwardly attempt to carve out independence from their families (and often become uncomfortable with public displays of affection), this was never the case with Christian.

A friend of ours, Noreen, witnessed this and said to Christopher, "I once saw Danielle and Christian shopping at the mall when he was on break and was touched by how affectionate he was with his mom! And I remember sitting with you at a football game when he was marching, and when the band ran up the steps to go to the concession stand, he made sure to stop and say hello to you, Chris. None of the other kids were doing that." It warms our hearts and fills us with pride to know that others recognized Christian's uniqueness—long before he became ill.

Christian would shower us with love, hugs, and kisses at social and school events—or even while walking through a store or at Sunday Mass. Christian was not afraid of beating his own drum and expressing love to everyone, nor was he afraid of all that he set out to do in life. I believe that that is why he was a magnet for so many. People desired to be part of the radiant love and joy he emanated, as well as the comfortable individualism he exemplified. That is why he had so many appreciators. He had a wide network of people whom he met through various contexts who loved, adored, and respected him—and who stayed in touch, always.

When he was first diagnosed with his rare liver cancer, the Rosary Gals prayer group in front of our house asked what Christian wanted them to pray for and he requested that they, "Pray for people with cancer who do not have access to the kind of medical, family, and social support that I do, and for those people suffering alone with cancer." He told us that he was glad that God chose him for this burden to bear, and if given the choice, he would never give it to anyone else because that would mean that another person would have to suffer. He also told his doctors at the onset of his diagnosis, and repeatedly throughout the journey of his treatment, that he was happy to be of medical service for them. He expressed an eager interest to help others and contribute to the discovery of better treatments, and a potential cure for cholangiocarcinoma.

Christian remained humble and appreciative. He often expressed feeling awkward about the materially comfortable life that we provided for him. He had a strong sense of commitment to living a materially minimalistic life. He routinely shopped at Goodwill and at porch and garage sales, and was so proud of his two-dollar sweatshirts.

Midway through his year of treatment, after receiving his chemotherapy infusion, Christian one day asked to go walking with me on the grounds of La Roche College. We walked through the trails, prayed at the graves of all the nuns on the grounds, and sat talking on a bench with a canopy of trees surrounding us. Christian wanted me to know that he was okay with his burden and death, that he was grateful for all that his father and I had given him in his lifetime, and that he had lived a wonderful life: He was ready to meet Christ.

He also reminded me that his sister and brother were going to need me to be strong and loving for them, once he was gone. He assured me that everything was going to be fine. He told me not to be upset, angry, or bitter and to never lose the love, joy, and zest for God and the life he knew I had. This particular point was of great concern for him—the health of my spirit, my ability to survive, and my potential to experience happiness in a life he knew I could settle for living with a hardened heart. He knew that the latter life could easily be lived by a mother experiencing the loss of a child. My awareness of this was important to him and he revisited the thought. He knew how incredibly hurt I would be if he were to die, and he extracted a promise from me that I would forever remain myself and not be angry or bitter. He comforted me. I wanted to comfort *him*—but it was always Christian instinctively comforting *us*.

From the time of his diagnosis to his very last days, he would repeatedly assure us that everything was going to be alright. The last words he spoke (in response to me telling him that I loved him) were, "I love you *more*, I will pray for you, Mom." He once again assured us in his final hours that everything was going to be okay for us and not to worry.

Our beloved son was very, very sick for well over a year. It makes me nauseated to think of the enormous tumor that was growing in his liver, pressing into his stomach, spine, shoulder blades, lungs, and metastasizing throughout his body. Even Christian's most basic of functions became compromised: eating, breathing, sleeping, and sitting. Everything became uncomfortable and painful, yet Christian never complained. He didn't want to worry us. He truly knew that complaining would not accomplish anything—it was only wasted time and energy.

We had to insist upon taking Christian for more scans when his ability to walk became irregular. The scans confirmed that he had three broken vertebrae in his back and a broken scapula. He never told us how much physical pain he was in. He knew his fate and wanted to spend his last days on Earth with positivity, joy, and happiness—without adding additional work or worry than we were already faced with. His sweet self even apologized for his illness—as if there was the least reason for him to feel responsible for the circumstances. He wanted to be a bright and shining light during our family's darkest days. All he ever wanted was to bring to our family, his friends, and the world pure joy, love, light, and to please God.

Christian was extremely spiritual. We prayed and talked about God daily. He held onto his rosary beads for weeks. I reminded him that holding them is like holding the hand of our Blessed Mother. He made a point of telling us how much he loved us and that everything was going to be fine. He promised us that he would be in the stars, in heaven, and never too far from us. I asked him if he would be in Antares (his favorite star) and he replied, "Absolutely!"

Christian never gave up. While he seemed to know and accept his fate well before we could, he had continued to hope and leave open the chance for more time with all of us, or the likelihood of a miracle or a cure. We prayed for this but increasingly recognized and accepted the inevitable. Christian accepted his fate with grace, faith, appreciation for the privilege of life, wisdom, bravery, and exquisite sensitivity and concern for our struggle. He accepted it without complaints of his circumstances, but rather with love and gratitude for all that he had been given in his lifetime. He remained grateful for his family and friends and showed the utmost respect for the medical personnel working hard to care for him and aid in his comfort as much as possible.

In Christian's final weeks of life, we had to rush him to more radiation therapy to prevent him from becoming paralyzed. There was a cancerous tumor growing in his neck, causing tremendous pain. Once again, Christian didn't complain. He simply ordered a neck heating pad from Amazon for himself without troubling any of us. The tumor was severe, and doctors warned us that if we did not address it immediately, he would be paralyzed from the neck down and would not be able to stay at home with his family and dogs in his final days on Earth. Still, during these final weeks, he abstained from complaining. We kept praying and used holy water to bless him. We used relics of saints to place on his body and prayed to them for intercessions.

Christian attended Mass regularly until he was not able to walk or travel any longer. He would then watch Mass on television. He remained humble and spiritual. The last few weeks before he passed, he wasn't able to swallow his pills or even the smallest amounts of liquid. His mouth was bright red, raw, and irritated from dehydration and the trial drug that he had taken previously. We would moisten his mouth with a damp sponge. Amazingly, he still didn't complain. He never made you pity him. Instead, he tried to see the humor in every situation and find the joy. And love—love was by far the greatest gift he bestowed on all. He knew that love conquers all matters of the heart and spirit. He wouldn't even allow us to refer to his cancer negatively. He was adamant that it was "his honorable adversary," and he "did not want to show it disrespect." Was Christian's love for all living things so great that he even respected the cancer growing within him? Indeed, it seemed he was incapable of harboring any ill feelings, even toward the worst things.

His infectious smile didn't disappear during his illness: He laughed, made jokes, wrote music, and started to write a children's book about his beloved dog, Maple. He still danced and greeted his friends and family with compassion, kindness, respect, and above all things—with love. When the cancer had spread to his bones (his spine, femur, hip, and shoulders), he would often ask us, *what's good about today?* It remained his daily reminder to us all that we had to focus on all that is good within each day, that life is short, and to make the very most of it. He kept showing us that time should not be wasted on judging others. Instead, finding the goodness in each day, saying "I love you" daily, hugging your family, and talking to a stranger or someone with a different life experience than yours were the essential things in life. He taught us to listen. He taught us to learn about others. He taught us to show respect to all. But most of all, he taught us not to fear death. He reminded us that the only way to the Father is through Jesus, and he loved Jesus. Of course, he wanted more time on Earth, but Christian understood that his commitment was to pay all the love and kindness that he received forward to others. He was never bitter or afraid of dying.

On the drive to his final treatment (August 17th, 2021—the last time he would leave our family home), he told us in the car, "Mom and Dad, all I ever wanted was to do kind things for people." We told him that we would continue to do just that for him, in his name. We told him about the Legacy Fund through the Pittsburgh Foundation that we were creating in his honor. He was happy and thought it was a great idea, and he expressed his love for theater and space and that perhaps we could do something for kids who did not have the opportunities to participate in camps that taught these things. He wanted us to help young kids learn about the beauty of the night skies and create an eagerness to learn more about the stars after his death. He also expressed his love for nature, animals, and his beloved church in the Strip District, Saint Stanislaus Kostka.

Even as he moved to a full, open realization that he would die, he embraced our plans for memorializing him. He spoke so eloquently about his love and appreciation for us and everything that we did for him in his life, especially during the last year. He was grateful for our attempt to work fervently to save him and ultimately make him as comfortable as possible. He had a remarkable sensitivity toward us, even showing great enthusiasm for the unfolding plans we spoke about to memorialize him.

His memory and loving way will always be alive as a blessing to all who knew him and those who heard his story. He trusted in God, and he remained hopeful throughout his entire illness. He prayed fervently, went to the church for sacramental blessings twice, and held relics of saints, yet he was smart enough to understand the devastation that his illness was causing his body. That is why he continued to spread hope and love to others. He knew his time on Earth was dissipating and he had to share all the love that God gave him with everyone he encountered.

Here he was, a very young man dying, yet he brought everyone around him joy and enormous love and peace. His gifts were priceless—the sort you never forget because they made you feel so good, so loved, and so important. And without judgment, he showered all with his beautifully kind love. There are no coincidences. Everything happens for a reason. We believe that God chose Christian for this enormous burden because he was already strong and firm in his belief. He was popular and dynamic—how could he *not* choose Christian? If you truly want to encourage compassion, wouldn't you shine a light that leads to Christian's guidance?

On the eve of Christian's first chemotherapy, after people started finding out about his diagnosis, more than one hundred gathered in front of our house to pray and sing songs for Christian. On Christmas Eve, many people gathered again in front of the house to pray and sing songs of Christmas love. And once again, on the day of his passing, over a hundred people came to light candles, pray, and sing songs of praise to God. We never asked anyone to come on any of these occasions. Each time they did so on their own accord. They came because of Christian—they came because of his love and light and hope, and moreover, they came to seek his faithful connection to God.

For me, I lost my son and my firstborn child. I lost the one person on Earth about whom I can honestly say never brought me anything but joy, peace, and love. He loved me unconditionally—with all my faults. At my weakest moments (mostly because of the deterioration of his health and the realization of his impending death), he comforted me and told me that everything was going to be alright. He told me that he had lived a wonderful life filled with blessings for which he'd be forever grateful. He thanked me for all the hard work and the sacrifices I made to give him so much. He told me he was ready to meet Christ and again, had me promise that I would not be angry, upset, or change all that was good in my heart and soul because of his circumstances.

I have never in my lifetime known a person at any stage of life, let alone such a young person, so brave and faithful in the face of such utter chaos and imminent death—so at peace with it. I cannot imagine any other person who would not complain when they had so much to complain or be angry about. And I have never had a relationship in my life where someone loved me so deeply and unconditionally, teaching me so much while accepting me just the way I am without any judgment. Christian's love was pure—it was perfect. He taught me how to live. He taught me how to not fear death. Because of Christian's journey and the great love that I witnessed, I believe now more than I did at the time of his birth that God always had a great plan for Christian. And He gave Christian the tools of hope and a beautiful future here on Earth and in heaven.

Even through all I have experienced in watching my "beauty full" and brilliant, loving, empathetic gem of a son physically wither away in the force of this illness over the past year, I still have hope in God. I still trust His plan for our family and, especially, our heavenly Christian.

In November 2018, Christian traveled to Rome to visit the Vatican. He was in awe of all its beauty. This had been during his semester abroad, studying in Prague. When he returned home from that semester, he gave us rosary beads made from rose petals from the Vatican gift store. We did not use them until his diagnosis two years later, and now, we fervently pray the rosary daily (sometimes more than once). I love my rosary beads from my son—they serve as a beautiful connection to our Blessed Holy Mother and the Holy Bible. The rosary beads, with their fragrant sweet scent of roses, are a most cherished gift from Christian.

In my eyes, Christian was and will be forever the most virtuous soul I have known: "I will pray for you, Mom and Dad. I love you *more*."

## *Online Media Impressions*

I think Danielle's words above capture so much of their unique mother and son connection. They remind me of the days shortly after his terminal diagnosis when Christian engaged with other cancer patients and survivors on the online platform Reddit (ShavingFoam, 2020). Imagine: You are 22, you just graduated from college, and now you are ready to start your life as an adult. How exciting it should be!

But this was not the journey for Christian. He was dealing with a fatal diagnosis and despite his discomfort and shattered dreams, his main concern was about his family. On the site, he posted these remarkable words:

> 22 years old with Cholangiocarcinoma:
>
> Not sure how to start this, thanks for allowing me space to talk in your community. I've been suffering from horrible back pain all year, and here I was thinking it was all my time at the computer doing online classes giving me back pain! According to my doctors, I've got a 10 x 15 cm tumor on my liver, pressing into my diaphragm and stomach [with] regional spread to lymph nodes. Been through one round of chemo and getting my port put in tomorrow. It's been a crazy three weeks for me.
>
> I guess it's my family that's the hardest part. This year was supposed to be a big deal for me—graduating college and moving out into the world and whatnot, but instead, I'm stuck at home in lots of pain, getting bizarre (to me) medical treatments and generally just laying around exhausted. I can handle that sort of thing, life is full of these types of challenges after all, but it's my family that makes it tough: My mother and father have to see me like this, my younger siblings have watched their brother turn into what seems like an old man.

I guess what I'm trying to say is that, even though I am the one suffering through cancer, it's seeing the way it affects those around me that hurts the most. I hate feeling like I'm ruining everything for them. Like their perfect life was derailed because I decided to get a disease that statistically I shouldn't have!!! I worry that, if I die, this will affect them in ways I can't imagine. Maybe I'm just being vain, but I really just wanted to vent.

Let me know if any of you have been through something like this, and if anyone else here has experience with Intra-Hepatic Bile Duct cancer. I could use some pointers because I'm new at this. Much love. XOXOXO

What hit me the hardest from this post is that despite this remarkably caring and humble message by Christian—who merely didn't want to burden his own family with his concerns about them and attempted to engage with strangers for "some pointers" to deal with his mental pain—the responses to his words were far from encouraging or positive. Yet, he remained positive for the year that followed his diagnosis. Christian was seeking advice on how to navigate his diagnosis for the best of his *family*. He wasn't worried about himself—he was concerned for his mother, father, brother, and sister. The heartache he felt while watching our sadness must have overpowered the excruciating physical pain he endured.

Now, if that is not noble, angelic, virtuous, and unselfishly humble—what is?

# Living a Meaningful Life

Christian always cared deeply for others. Even during the most difficult moments of his illness, he was more concerned about others than himself. He never wanted anyone to worry or feel burdened by his own struggles. It was a testament to his selflessness and unwavering love for those around him. Christian truly was a remarkable soul.

He would sit in chemotherapy weekly with people three times his age and they would complain about their cancer, illness, and life. But he would try to encourage them to be positive and find the good in their days. He could have closed his curtain and sat privately for his chemotherapy, but he wanted to help those around him find ways to navigate their illness in a more positive light. He never complained or remarked about 80-year-old men complaining about having a less devastating cancer than his own and he never shared that his cancer was terminal. Christian deliberately chose to have a high-quality life and use his time spent on this Earth to help others, not wallow in his own sorrows. That was how he navigated his life.

On countless occasions, I would hear whispers from his friends in his inner circle that Christian would always be "fine" because he was none other than Christian Cochran. He did not want to burden his friends with the seriousness of his illness and cause them any worry. Such remarks became the norm, as it was unfathomable for anyone to believe that Christian could ever fall ill and depart from this world. He possessed an extraordinary nature that made him too special, too unique, too compassionate, too talented, too kind, too generous, too remarkable, too humorous, too intelligent, too empathetic, and above all, too overflowing with *love*! He was simply so perfect and worthy—that nothing as terrible as a rare, terminal cancer diagnosis (with only a two to three percent survival rate after its spread beyond the bile ducts) would take him from this Earth (American Cancer Society, n.d.).

Despite this, Christian strived to find purpose in everyday life. After his diagnosis, he still worked his full-time salesman job for ADP. I think that he had every right to rage at his fate and the injustice that crossed his path (and no one would have blamed him for that), yet he still retained his youthful and peaceful spirit. Having to deal with the excruciating pain that this rare cancer inflicted on him did not stop him at all. Many other people would be emotionally and physically numbed, but he continued to work eight hours a day for six months while receiving heavy chemotherapy and a range of high-level drugs running through his veins. That takes a different level of grit and stamina—something that many healthy and able-bodied people would fail to accomplish. I hope that this example encourages others to follow his admirable work ethic.

His aunt, Heather, had this to say in her endearing letter:

> From the time of his diagnosis at the close of last summer, when the Jewish Bible says the old year ends and the new year begins, to his passing—which happened at the exact same time the next year—he was sweet, funny, determined, hardworking, and inconceivably brave.
>
> When I first saw him at this time last September, just days after his diagnosis, he looked very thin, and I was afraid for him and for all of us who loved him. He was resting on a bench in the garden at my brother and sister-in-law's house, and I said to him, "Christian, I love you and you're going to beat this." He looked at me and said, "Don't worry, Heathie. It's going to be okay." I repeated, "Yes, because you're going to get well," and Christian said, "Heathie, whatever happens, it's going to be okay."
>
> It was like he was the one comforting me, and reassuring me of some deeper spiritual truth.

When he passed and we visited the nurses and doctors at Hillman Cancer Center, a nurse came running to me in the hallway in tears and said, "Mr. Cochran, you have no idea of the many lives that your son has changed in this building." The receptionist at Hillman CC wrote us a letter after Christian's death and said that she felt guilty for always being so happy and looking forward to when Christian would come for treatments because he brightened the rooms and moods of the people there.

Christian was determined to live every day to the fullest, right to the end. He would always ask Danielle at the end of most days during his final year, *"What's good about today?"* And despite his deteriorating condition, he kept inspiring others and remained focused on other people instead of himself. Besides spending his days focusing on work, he shared his beautiful self with his loved ones, including Rachael, the love of his life who stood by him until his last day. He spent his time with his friends and family, and even worked with me to establish a foundation that would help others around the world who are facing the same challenges brought on by this aggressive cancer. Christian did his best to let the world know that he would be of service to those less fortunate than him. It remained his final passion and desire until his last breath. The lessons and insights our family has learned from his unworldly spirit go beyond me.

## A Legacy of Resilience

When we look at resilience, we realize that facing challenges entails bravery, courage, and strength. We all have our challenges. And we all respond differently to them. And we all know that these challenges can be difficult to overcome. I have found that resilience grows as we journey through life. When I look at Christian's way of coping with obstacles, I become silent. Perhaps that is exactly what we need to do when we observe a great spirit facing its worst enemies. What did David do in the face of Goliath's strength? He relied on his trust in something stronger than him... Maybe sometimes, we need to see how others face demons, more challenging than our own, in order to garner the muscle we need to overcome them.

Some of the last Instagram posts Christian made were photos tinged with a sense of humor, which he always maintained despite his cancer. Christian loved the '80s and all that the era of "disco and bright lights" encapsulated. In one photo, he posted himself in a wheelchair (because he could no longer walk). He captioned it, "Walkman? Not lately!" In the photo, you can see he's holding his old Sony Walkman music player in his hands.

## Concluding Thoughts: Inspired by Christian

A few ideas that come to mind as I think of Christian's courageous effort are as follows:

- Having positive intentions.

- Contentment.
- Self-care.
- Finding purpose.
- Igniting joy.
- Complimenting others.
- Smiling.

Complaints cannot accomplish anything. In the face of adversaries, we should instead do the following:

- Garner meaningful connections that enhance confidence and foster trust.
- Embrace a life of gratitude. Keep a journal. Write a self-compassion letter. Do random acts of kindness.
- Downplay negativity. Shift our thinking. Refrain from bitterness.
- Love.

Maintain your zest for life. Keep going and never give up. Hold on to hope. Keep your faith strong. Embrace life without fear of death.

Chapter 7:

# Between Hope and Acceptance

*Grief can be the garden of compassion. If you keep your heart open through everything, your pain can become your greatest ally in your life's search for love and wisdom.* –Rumi

During Christian's illness, family members—including myself—would try to comfort him and make sure he knew that it was all going to be okay. Ironically, during these moments, it always ended up that Christian would be the comforter to us, telling us that everything would be okay and not to worry. Perhaps that is why when he was diagnosed and his mother said that she was sorry, by expressing how she wanted to take the diagnosis away from him and bear it herself, he responded without hesitation, "I would never give this cancer to anyone and I accept that it's my burden to carry for Christ. I would and could never watch anyone else suffer this illness." He was adamant about this: There was no wavering.

## Grieving as a Family

Grieving happens throughout loss—not only after it. There is an onset of grief, the path of grief, and the aftermath of grief. Each phase comes with its unique challenges. Christian's siblings still struggle to express their grief as the emotions overwhelm them. As a parent, I respect their ways, and I cannot impose my way of dealing with grief on them. The relationship that I shared with Christian is very different from the one Danielle and his siblings had with him. To each of us, the grieving process is a slow and painful journey of our own. It has been a grieving journey since the day of his diagnosis. Of course, as a family unit and with the support of extended family members and the wider community, we feel strengthened. But our individual paths remain distinctly unique.

Let me illustrate the effect of heightened emotions during the grieving journey before loss with the following story. A few months before his passing, on a pretty summer's day, Christian and Danielle went shopping. They'd spent a relaxing and joyful day together, finding cassette tapes for his new Walkman, among other things. Christian insisted on driving (despite his severe back pain). Danielle was extremely proud of his courage and ability despite the pain.

They drove past the church and down the hill toward the dog park. As they approached the park, Danielle saw a doe and her three fawns appearing from the woods. The spotted fawns were frolicking and joyfully playing with each other.

A few minutes earlier, Christian had put on some Peter Gabriel, and they were listening to his song *Don't Give Up*. The moment's beauty was enhanced by the song's lyrical meaning and nature unfolding so majestically in front of them. They both started crying until their mutual tears became moments of laughter as emotions overwhelmed them both. They were laughing through their tears.

Danielle looked at the deer and saw that one of the fawns had disappeared into the woods, leaving the mother and the other two babies behind. It was like watching Christian, Kate, and Nick playing together under the watchful eye of their mother. And then Christian left them, running into the woods.

The way that Danielle recounted this event touched me deeply. The significance of those deer, the mother with her babies, the theme song of never giving up, and the aching awareness of the reality that lay ahead were enough to set my emotions going in all directions. During the onset period of grief, despite the glimmering moments of joy enticed by Christian's vibrant spirit, our lives were weighted with feelings. We supported each other as much as we could, but overwhelm set in in countless times.

Grief is an indescribable hardship.

It's a world that exposes you to something you never knew existed, and it's painful to the core and beyond. It immediately turns all your beliefs and thoughts about life and loss into something catastrophically different. How do we best deal with such pain? Well, the best way to navigate it is to stay in the present moment: living life as it is unfolding and being there for yourself and others. It means taking time to enjoy and savor the little things. To celebrate the pockets of joy as they come. It helps knowing that we will be reunited with our loved ones one day. Truly, nothing is promised to us in this life, so love the beautiful moments you share with loved ones fully. Love them unconditionally, express your love for them, and tell them *what* you love about them.

The other way to deal with grief is to do things for other people—and animals, for that matter. It feels wonderful to help those in need. No matter how small or big the need, it all matters collectively and helps you to find the greatest joy. It could be a kind word, a smile, a compliment to a stranger, or helping others during their most challenging times. We enjoy the opportunity to help other young adults who struggle financially and emotionally when they are given a cancer diagnosis. The Christian Cochran Legacy Fund of the Pittsburgh Foundation supports these young adults by gifting those in need monthly with a "necessity bag" filled with essentials, to help them with the burden of navigating the difficult financial and mental journey of terminal illness.

This is something that our "beauty full" Christian was advocating for, and it warms our hearts while giving us purpose to help and honor his wishes. From this, we have learned that finding a purpose—and passionately chasing that purpose—actively transforms our pain into love. That's what helps us navigate the journey of grief and losing our most precious Christian. Christian is our role model. Just imagine all the good we could do in this world if we just loved and cared about each other more—and expressed it more often.

# Christian's Wish

As Christian's health deteriorated in the weeks preceding his death, I vividly remember driving him to the hospital on August 2nd. Despite the short distance, the journey felt interminable as I desperately tried to get him to the doctor's office. During that agonizing drive, I mustered the courage to ask Christian about his wishes, wanting to ensure that I could honor him even after he departed this earthly realm. To my delight, Christian expressed a desire to give back to the Church, which had provided him with immense support throughout his life.

On that fateful trip to the hospital, Christian confided in me about a remarkable experience he had had. He spoke of being surrounded by joyful children, dancing and exuding happiness. I inquired whether this was a dream or a vision to which he responded that it was happening at that very moment. His words were not the ramblings of medication-induced delirium, but rather a heartfelt testament to the presence of these ethereal beings. I couldn't help but believe they were preparing for Christian's arrival in heaven, eagerly anticipating his entrance with a grand celebration.

Visions before death are a common occurrence. Many caregivers and family members have given evidence of this while looking after palliative care patients. These situations are quite common in the weeks leading up to the death of a loved one. Carolyn Quach-Huynh, a nurse from Crossroads Hospice and Palliative Care, says, "It's also not always a vision. It can be a deceased spouse or parent appearing in dreams. Or a familiar smell—like cigars or a certain perfume" (Crossroads Hospice, 2017, para 4). There is no need to feel concerned about this. One can simply acknowledge and support them as these visions are often very comforting for the person. Having visions of someone "waiting for them on the other side" can provide a feeling of peace.

After arriving at the hospital, we were soon ushered into our usual room, and Dr. Raj, Christian's oncologist, requested a private conversation with me. He delivered the heartbreaking news that there was nothing more they could do for Christian. We had to focus on ensuring his remaining time on this Earth was as comfortable as possible. Although I knew deep down that this was the reality, *some part of me didn't want to hear that*. However, the doctor thought patient transparency was crucial.

We returned to the room and I held one of Christian's hands while Dr. Raj held the other. Christian looked directly into the doctor's eyes with his beautifully gentle gaze; expressing gratitude for his care and acknowledging the doctor's genuine kindness. It was an emotionally challenging moment, yet Christian's composure and awareness of his circumstances were awe-inspiring: He had made peace with his fate long before that instant.

Armed with this knowledge, we left the hospital, determined that Christian would spend his final moments at home, surrounded by love from his family and pets. We arranged for a hospital bed to be placed in our living room where countless memories had been made. It was the heart of our home where we had gathered for TV and movie nights, and celebrated every holiday since our children were young. Little did we know, throughout our years of happiness in this space, that this room would become the setting for our worst nightmare: a reality that still feels surreal.

I won't delve into the painful details of what transpired during that last month with Christian. It was an experience no parent should ever have to endure. However, what I can say is that Christian was constantly enveloped in love. Our family—including Danielle, Kate, Nicholas, Rachael, and myself, along with Christian's Aunt Bridget, Uncle David, and their son Grant—were a constant presence by his side. I set up a blow-up mattress next to Christian's bed in the living room where I slept so I could be in physical contact with him. Danielle would read stories to Christian while lying next to him, and Rachael would also take turns lying next to him, forming a makeshift giant bed by pushing the hospital bed against the couch.

Approximately two weeks before Christian's passing, his phone unexpectedly rang. Without hesitation, I answered the call only to discover Christian's Pittsburgh-based agent on the other end. They were eager to inform him of an exciting opportunity—a new movie set to be filmed in Pittsburgh, with Christian being deemed the perfect fit for a leading role. In the brief exchange that followed, I attempted to convey the reason for Christian's unavailability. However, my son overheard our conversation and mustered the strength to interject, his voice filled with determination: "Dad, do they understand my circumstances? Please, inform them that I just need a little more time." It astounded me how, despite his weakened state, he clung to the belief that he could overcome his affliction. It also reminded me of his unique concept of time: Perhaps he said that to relay a message of kindness and gratitude for the magnificent offer they presented. Christian never lost hope; he refused to surrender. His indomitable spirit persisted, propelling him forward with the conviction that he could outlast the grasp of his merciless disease.

We made a point of reminding Christian of the profound impact he had on all of us and how he made our lives better. From the moment of his diagnosis, we needed to maintain a connection with our church, St. Stanislaus Kostka in Pittsburgh, and our beloved priest, Father Nick Vaskov. Father Nick blessed Christian during the week of his diagnosis and remained an integral part of our family throughout our arduous year-long journey. In those final weeks, Father Nick even came to our home, providing solace and spiritual guidance during our darkest hours.

I vividly remember a poignant moment during Christian's final week of life. It was around 4 a.m. when his breathing became more strained and constricted. I immediately summoned our entire family to gather around Christian, knowing deep down that this could be his departure from our world, at least for now. In the dimly lit room, we lit candles and encircled his bed, each of us taking turns expressing our profound gratitude for having him in our lives.

We shared heartfelt stories about the immense joy he brought, not only to us but to countless others. Danielle and I poured out our infinite love, thanking him for the boundless happiness, affection, and laughter he bestowed upon us. Nicholas expressed his gratitude for Christian's unwavering support and role-modeling. Kate spoke of their deep connection and the pure love she held for his kindness. And Rachael repeatedly professed her profound love for him.

This circle of love and appreciation continued for a couple of hours, enveloping Christian in warmth and affection. Then, at around 6 a.m., something incredible happened: Christian's eyes fluttered open, and we all leaned in closer, gazing at his angelic face and mesmerizing brown eyes. Confused, he looked at us and asked, "What's going on?" We responded in a choir of voices, "Well, we called the priest, thinking this was your moment." With a mischievous smile and a hint of humor, Christian replied, "Tell Father Nick to save the trip." Even in the face of adversity, Christian managed to evoke laughter from all of us. It was a testament to his indomitable spirit and the light he carried within, even as his time with us drew to a close.

Father Nick still paid us a visit at our home that same day after being called. His purpose: to spend precious moments with Christian and administer his last rites. I observed Christian whispering intently, his words shrouded in mystery. To this day, I ponder the nature of their conversation, eagerly awaiting the day I reunite with my son to finally uncover the truths exchanged on that fateful day. I'm certain their discussion revolved around the essence of compassion and caring for others—a testament to Christian's unwavering concern for the well-being of those around him.

Christian's tenacity stemmed from the endless love that resided within him. His heart, seemingly boundless in size, overflowed with affection for life itself. Every breath he took was with profound adoration for this world and the abundant beauty it offered to each and every one of us. Even before his illness consumed him, Christian would tirelessly extol the wonders of the world and the remarkable individuals who inhabited it. I have yet to encounter a single soul on this vast planet who did not hold Christian in high regard. In fact, he was showered with love and adoration simply because of the immense love he unreservedly shared with others.

## The Final Goodbye

Christian's passing was a somber event. It happened on September 1st at 12:38 pm amid a dark and rainy afternoon. The overcast sky seemed to reflect the collective sadness enveloping the world. I can't help but recall that day with clarity. First, I had a premonition that Christian would transition to the other side on Kate's birthday: that same September the first. It was as if fate wanted to emphasize the profound bond Christian shared with his siblings.

On that fateful morning, Dr. Sumaiya Zaidi (one of Christian's doctors) arrived to see him. Before that, she had visited our home, providing us with nourishment and spending precious moments with Christian. This doctor's life had been profoundly transformed by Christian. She yearned to be near him and was present alongside our family when Christian departed on that distressing day. She was like an angel sent to our family, bearing witness, like the rest of us, to Christian's passing. With poignant certainty, she uttered, "Christian not only taught us how to live but also how to die." She immediately embraced my son Nicholas. It was as if she knew with certainty she needed to be there with Nicholas and I confided in her that it was Christian, nudging her to embrace my younger son.

Danielle confessed to me how fast her heart was beating that last month of his life. She wanted it to be different, saying the following words:

> I wish I could have been the first one to greet Christian in heaven and kiss him and hug him ever so tightly, wrapped and protected in my arms, after having lived a very long, happy life.
>
> Why? Why? Why could that not be?
>
> It's an awful thing to lose a child: The worst pain, so strong. There are no earthly words to convey the feeling.

From the day of his diagnosis to the day of his passing, only one year had elapsed. We have a photo of him in the hospital on Labor Day 2020 after being diagnosed, with a big smile and a thumbs up. One year later, he passed on his beloved sister's birthday. They were very close, only 15 months apart, and almost like twins. They grew up together and loved each other deeply.

We believe that this is one more blessing for the family. The anniversary of Christian's passing is not exclusively a sad day because we celebrate Kate's birthday then.

I'd like to share with you Danielle's aching thoughts about Christian's passing, as follows:

> I remember the morning of the day you died. You were trying so hard to stay with us. You were fighting for your life. You didn't want to leave us because you loved us all so much and you knew how much it was going to hurt us when you died.
>
> You used every ounce of strength to open your eyes and I saw through them into your heart and soul. I saw how much you loved me and your family. You hadn't opened your eyes like that for days and days.
>
> I told you how much I loved you and what an amazing son you are.
>
> It was a gift and blessing that I was able to be with you and hold you in your last weeks, days, hours, minutes, and moments here on Earth. I brought you into this world—close to me, holding and kissing you—and you left this world with me lying close to you—holding and kissing you.
>
> It was surreal and awful having you taken away after death. I watched you part—up the gentle slope of our street and then disappearing with two strange men in a minivan. It was awful.
>
> Then I saw your sweet smiling face—you were skipping—appearing up over the gentle slope of the sidewalk—happy as can be—just like you had done for so many years walking home from the bus stop, pleasantly thrilled and happy to be home with your family.

After the tragic loss of Christian, Danielle and I faced the daunting task of gathering our thoughts and organizing a memorial to honor our beloved son. I vividly remember a heartfelt conversation I had with Christian in our living room during those last two weeks. Tears streamed down my face as I clung to Christian, pouring out my love for him and my unbearable fear of losing him. Amid my anguish, he gently caressed my head and reassured me, saying, "Don't worry, Dad. Everything will be alright." During that conversation, Christian posed a question that touched my heart deeply. "Dad, where do you think my memorial will be?" Without hesitation, I responded, "Our cherished church, St. Stanislaus." A smile graced Christian's face as he responded, "Cool, I adore that place."

And so it was decided.

On September 11th, 2021, Christian's memorial took place at St. Stanislaus, a historic Polish church nestled in the heart of Pittsburgh. Established in 1873, this sacred place had even been blessed by the presence of the future Pope John Paul II himself during a visit in 1969. As he admired the beauty of the church, he likened it to the magnificent structures he had encountered in Poland. The Cardinal knelt in prayer before the Blessed Sacrament and later paid his respects at the Side Altar of the Blessed Virgin Mary, which now houses a humble memorial dedicated to the Pope.

The day of Christian's memorial was one of overwhelming attendance. The church was brimming with mourners, to the point where people were directed to the balconies that were no longer utilized for services. It was an unprecedented sight, as the church staff attested that it was the largest gathering they had ever witnessed—likely one for the records of its long history. The following week, as I found myself in Pittsburgh's bustling business district, a stranger approached me, unaware that I had just emerged from the church. Curiosity gleamed in his eyes as he inquired about the massive crowds he had witnessed the previous week. He wondered if a prominent dignitary or a person of great influence had been laid to rest, as he had never seen such an extraordinary gathering of cars around the church. Little did he know that those crowds had come to pay their respects to my precious son. Both Danielle and I recall being approached by a woman who said, "I have never in my entire life seen such a diverse group of people gathered in one space." I believe this was her way of saying how people from all walks of life loved Christian—and that is because *he* loved *them*.

During the memorial service, our family occupied the first row, surrounded by loved ones. Father Nick presided over the ceremony, of course, and he spoke of Christian most radiantly and affectionately, illuminating the qualities that made him so special. Christian's memorial at St. Stanislaus on that September day was a testament to the profound impact he had on the lives of many. It was a gathering that spoke volumes about the love and admiration he had garnered, forever etching his memory in the hearts of all who attended.

Writing a eulogy remained a challenge. Writing one for your own son is nearly impossible. Writing a eulogy for a young man who touched the lives of so many people in a uniquely remarkable (and almost saintly) way felt beyond the bounds of possibility. Words become mere words laced on a string of sentences that fail to represent the true value of emotions.

I tried.

I was determined to deliver Christian's eulogy with utmost sincerity. I needed to encapsulate and share as much about Christian at that poignant moment as I could. Clutching a lucky coin from Christian's wallet, I sought solace and steadiness. Surprisingly, I managed to deliver the entire eulogy without shedding a tear. Before this moment, I had implored Christian to empower his family and protect us—including myself—during that crucial moment. As I started, something extraordinary occurred: A profound sense of tranquility and serenity washed over me. It felt as if Christian stood right beside me; his gentle touch infusing energy into my very being. Fear and worry dissipated as Christian urged me to be at my absolute best.

And so I was.

## *The Eulogy*

"We are such stuff as dreams are made on." –William Shakespeare, The Tempest: Act IV, Sc I.

For my son, Christian.

Shakespeare's words could never ring more true than they do for you, Christian. Preparing a eulogy for Christian is difficult—not only because it's a struggle to find the precise words, but also because there is so much to be said and my words are tied down to brevity. There's no capturing Christian's shimmering totality in a eulogy—all the fun, the light, and the love that he represented cannot be bound in words. But we're prepared to do the best we can do here today.

Christian was our first-born. Danielle and I were further blessed when Kate, and later Nicholas, joined us. Christian shared great bonds with his siblings and loved spending time with each of them. Christian and Kate (or Lady Kate, as he sometimes referred to her) were early compatriots. They were close in age and distinct in personality. From their first days, they formed a complementary, fabulous, and dynamic duo.

When Kate initially learned to speak, she was repeatedly heard saying something incomprehensible to Christian, accompanied by a tug of his arm. Eventually, we came to understand that she was saying "Me-you," as in an urging "Come on, me and you, let's do this thing or that." Christian usually obliged, though we suspect that he may have turned Kate down a time or two, if her plans were too mischievous!

When Nicholas joined us, Christian instantly assumed a protective role, gently stroking Nicholas' head the day he was born, commenting on his "tininess," and that he'd been waiting for Nicholas "all day." Young Christian was always missing Nicholas, often phoning home from the school office to confirm that Nicholas was there, safe and sound. Later, as they grew to be young adults, it was Christian who would often point out to the rest of us the emergence of Nick's "cool" factor—the clothes he wore, his offbeat sense of humor, and his unique manner. Christian would say about Nick, "Nick's so cool, he's just doing him."

Later, their cousin Grant joined the fray, evening out the number of participants and enlarging the group for fun homemade theater productions and contests, organized by Christian and Kate. Christian had a very strong, special, loving bond with his siblings, cousin Grant, and his Cochran cousins.

From earliest childhood, Christian put other peoples' needs before his own. To him, this was the natural order of things. He didn't grow into being a kind and caring soul—Christian was that person from the moment he was born.

He was one of the most charismatic, happy, energetic, and positive people you could ever hope to know. His brilliant, beaming smile and boundless energy were a source of joy, happiness, and comfort to all whose paths crossed his. He was empathetic, loving, and inclusive to everyone he encountered.

To meet him was to love him. Christian sparkled with his own brand of intense energy, like a trillion beams of light. When he walked into a room, you would immediately be drawn to him, with his twinkling brown eyes, his glorious head of curly brown hair, and his own inimitable, quirky style of dress. Indeed, he was handsome, turning heads at the age of three and—from what I observed as a dad—also at 23! Rachael, the love of Christian's life and his partner who stood by him throughout this year of trial and difficulty with a maturity and loyalty women of two or three times her age would be challenged to demonstrate, enjoyed his handsome looks. But she knew, like the rest of us, they were just the outer reflection of Christian's vibrant inner beauty and character.

Among his many great qualities, Christian possessed a shining intellect, including a photographic memory. His school participated in a mock United Nations (UN) project and Christian not only memorized every single flag of the world, but also memorized key points from each Wikipedia entry about each country in the UN. Foreign culture fascinated him. The simple act of packing a bag and going someplace excited him. He was not a materialistic person; experiences were far more important to him than possessions.

Christian's prodigious memory was invaluable in his acting career. It would usually only take a couple of read-throughs to get a script word-perfect. He loved to perform, throwing himself heart and soul into whatever role he had been called upon to play. Christian landed the lead role in many plays. His ability to convincingly portray characters from many walks of life was a testament to his empathetic nature. I'm glad he was able to begin to live his dream of acting on stage and screen, including his cameo as a young teen, in a major motion picture. His role in The Dark Knight Rises secured his spot in American film history.

On August 26th, 2020, Christian was diagnosed with a rare cancer of the liver, called cholangiocarcinoma. When we told him how sorry we were, as parents, that he had to have this awful disease, he replied, "It's okay, because if it was not me, then it would be someone else that would have to endure this struggle." Since the day of his diagnosis, to the moment he took his last breath, Christian never complained—not once—about his situation. He willingly accepted his extraordinary burden. Being an ironic humorist, his Instagram and Twitter feeds were filled with humor throughout this year. Even after his disease became advanced and he was near the end of his life, his wit was a sword he sharpened to confront the adversary that was attacking his physical body. To name an example: After the cancer had progressed to the point where he required a wheelchair, Christian—an amused fan of '80s culture—posted a picture of himself in the wheelchair wearing a headset and holding a Sony Walkman. Under it, he wrote: "Walkman? Not lately." As in WALK, MAN? Not lately. Some more social media examples are "A large part of emotional maturity is finally admitting that Holiday by Madonna is your favorite song (everyone goes through this...)," and beneath a photograph of his hand pulling an IV drip on a stand with wheels, "Walking the drug." As his very close friend, Allan, and others will attest, Christian maintained his sense of humor and his love of gaming throughout this challenging year.

Eventually, Christian's cancer went to his bones. Much of his spine, his femur, his hip, and his shoulders became involved. Amazingly, he never complained. He would often ask us all, what's good about today? It was his daily reminder to us all that we had to focus on all that is good within each day, and to make the very most of it.

Over the course of Christian's treatment, we visited several respected medical centers, among them Sloan Kettering, Johns Hopkins, Cleveland Clinic, and Massachusetts General. Out of the blue, about a month ago, I received a call from a nurse from one of these facilities. She began our discussion with an apology. She hoped I'd understand that her reason for contacting me was personal, rather than medical, and that she was departing from HIPAA regulations and protocol in reaching out to me. She explained that it had been her job to transport Christian within the hospital by wheelchair from one location to another and that along the way, it's customary to point out some art installations and public displays that are hoped to benefit the patients in some way. She explained that she was compelled to call me because of a life-changing experience she'd encountered with Christian.

She described speaking with him in the hour they spent together. What was unusual was that Christian spent the entire time talking about her: "He wanted me to feel comfortable," she said. "He wanted me to be happy. He asked me about my life and made me laugh. He told me how grateful he was to get to know me and to learn about my life. He wanted me to know how important I was and wanted me to have a great day filled with joy." The nurse cried on the phone with me. She said, "He didn't owe me anything, yet he gave me everything. There he was, in the worst situation a person can be in, and all he cared about was me."

This is one story among many in a similar vein.

In private moments I shared with Christian, I came to understand how important it was for him to be there for others who needed him. When he struggled, it was always about making sure he could give all of himself to others. If friends were coming to see him, it was vitally important to Christian that he would be there for them. Let's think about that... People were coming to comfort Christian, the young man who was dying, but he didn't want to focus on himself. Instead, he chose to channel his energy toward others. His deepest fears were not about pain and suffering—or imminent death—but rather that he might fail to bring joy to people's hearts.

After his diagnosis, Christian never stopped living and thriving. He remained motivated in the face of overwhelming adversity. He got a full-time job as a salesman at Automatic Data Processing (a human resources software company). For the first six months after his diagnosis, while on heavy chemotherapy and a range of other drugs, he did the work of a healthy grown man from a home office in our basement. I lack the words to convey my respect. Many able-bodied healthy adults would do well to emulate his work ethic.

Even before his illness, Christian packed so much into his life and touched many people in profoundly positive ways. He also filled this past year with his signature creativity as a composer and podcaster while continuing to work with his sister Kate to produce a podcast about a topic that he loved and enjoyed: It's called Space Night. His LoFi electronic music is on Soundcloud. He was an extroverted person who maintained a huge circle of friends from many different backgrounds and walks of life. I've lost track of how many close friends he had, but I know he made each one feel unique and valued. There was nothing superficial about his friendships. When Christian was your friend, he had a way of lightening your load.

During the journey of the past year, Christian's kindness to others was returned by a couple of doctors who deserve special salutations. Dr. Sumaiya Zaidi, our palliative care specialist, is a remarkable woman who guided us faultlessly along the way. You never hear of doctors of her stature making house calls, yet here she was, visiting Christian at home, and was even present weeping with us and embracing us when he died. Dr. Mark Yarchoan of Johns Hopkins regularly went above and beyond, walking with us on the tightrope between hope and acceptance. I'm extremely grateful that my sister-in-law, Bridget, and my brother-in-law, David, were part of what we called the "CC Advisory Group," and their participation in every aspect of Christian's care along with Danielle and myself.

Their help was invaluable, and we couldn't have achieved what we did without either of them.

Our community pulled together, supporting us through every trial we faced. Our friends and neighbors lightened our load, offering support on an ongoing basis, as did our fellow parishioners and clergy. It was humbling to see all of these good and kind people taking time out of their busy lives to lend us their strength, their love, and their insight. Christian placed his trust in Our Lord and His teachings and lived his life accordingly. He exemplified all that was Christ-like: humility, kindness, joy, gratitude, self-sacrifice, selflessness, courage, and above all—love.

Christian extracted promises from each of us that we would always look for the good in every day, and as I look out and see all of your shining faces, it is easy to see the good in this day. You each have your own memories of Christian, and you each carry a part of him that is entirely yours. He knew with certainty that if you looked for the good in each day, you would find it. It was important to him to let you know that he was not afraid of dying. It was just another experience, and he was sure it would not be the last. On September 1st, 2021, Christian peacefully passed into God's loving embrace...

Christian's extraordinary devotion to others, his easygoing humility, his humor, his ability to comfort us even as he was the one facing mortality, all set him apart. He would never have claimed the mantle of sainthood (and had it been suggested, might have laughed and joked about the idea on Twitter), but in his way, I believe Christian was a 21st century saint. His courage and his selflessness, while confronting death at such a tender age, were heroic, even though he would not have seen it that way. Bravely, with love and humor, he walked its difficult path and uplifted the rest of us. With all that was extraordinary about him, Christian considered himself to be just a regular guy. But to my mind, that's exactly what made him a star.

Another snippet from Shakespeare: "And our little life is rounded with a sleep" (Tearle, 2021).

Christian, each of us who had the privilege of your light shining upon us knows that the only thing that was little about your life was its duration. You packed so much of your love, your grace, and your brilliant mind into your 23 years. Christian, you are so deeply loved by us all. Always. Rest in Peace.

After the memorial, as our family made our way outside the church, the bustling streets came alive with vibrant energy. People formed lines, eager to exchange a few words with Danielle and me. Some interactions were brief, while others lingered longer. Tears flowed freely from many, while others offered sympathetic expressions. Once again, I felt Christian's presence embracing me, keeping me composed and alert. Despite the overwhelming crowd, I miraculously recalled every person's name that day. It's worth mentioning that I am typically terrible with names, yet, on this occasion, I possessed an uncanny ability to identify and remember each individual who approached me. Their names rolled off my tongue effortlessly, and I even knew their personal stories or how they were connected to Christian. Even his extensive circle of friends were familiar to me.

I vividly remember a woman who approached me, accompanied by two others. She introduced herself as a professor from Christian's university, bringing along two students who had known him from class. Not only did I recall her name, but I also remembered the names of those students. Her presence was unexpected, as she followed the Islamic faith and had never attended a Christian religious event before. However, Christian's profound impact on her life and his overwhelming kindness inspired her to be present one more time. Driving two hours to be there, she shared how Christian's character had left an indelible mark on her. She spoke of the uniqueness of his kindness and how he had touched her soul.

This was not an isolated incident. Throughout the day, people from various corners of the world approached me, recounting stories of how Christian had transformed their lives. From brief encounters lasting mere minutes to lifelong connections, each person had a story to share.

One particular instance stands out in my memory. While attending an event celebrating Christian's life (separate from the memorial), a transgender woman approached me. Tearfully, she introduced herself as someone who had known Christian. She struggled to maintain composure, but her gratitude and admiration for Christian were palpable. She expressed how he had been the only person to show her genuine love and kindness during her difficult journey of transition: "At the most challenging period of my life, Christian made me feel important and valued in this world," she tearfully confided.

I do not know how to bid farewell to a loved one—I cannot tell you how it's done. I did not know how to do it when our beautiful son had to go. I'm still learning. All I know is that it's an endless, painful process: There is no farewell, there is only a wave to indicate some sense of letting go. Perhaps that is my river. Perhaps that is the flow that I have to follow as a father—and perhaps my loving wife and beloved children are learning that too.

## Concluding Thoughts: Inspired by Christian

We cannot escape grief. It will cross our paths at some point. How do we face our grief?

- Step by step.
- Navigate.
- Take hands.
- Share and support.
- Make peace.
- Remain kind.
- Remain hopeful.
- Make someone smile.
- Make someone feel unique.

- Make someone feel valued.
- And do not be afraid of dying.

# Chapter 8:

# A Lasting Impact

*One moment can change a day, one day can change a life, and one life can change the world.* –The Buddha

We said our goodbyes. We started saying them on that life-changing day of his diagnosis. And we still haven't completed them. Christian will always be with us. His profound spirit is with us in every second that we share as a family. How could it be any different? He left his everlasting impact and legacy with us—there is no way that it can be lost.

## Christian's Lasting Legacy

We sent our lovingly supportive *CaringBridge* community the following message on September 6th, 2021:

Dear friends and family,

We regret to inform you of the passing of our sweet, loving Christian. Thank you for all the love, prayers, and support along the way this past year. Every act of kindness was greatly appreciated.

We have established the Christian Cochran Legacy Fund through the Pittsburgh Foundation to carry on Christian's gift of kindness, love for the arts, animals, and much more. We are very appreciative of your kindness and desire to better the world out of respect for Christian and in his honor. With love and gratitude, Cochrans All.

Almost a year later, we organized the first annual 3k *What's GOOD About TODAY?* nature hike in memory of our beautiful, loving

Christian, which was held at the North Park in Allegheny County, PA. We hoped to encourage people to slow down and appreciate nature, as well as all the goodness that surrounds us. By that time, Christian's daily reminder of *what's good about today* had become a powerful motto for all of us to focus on all that is good within each day. Through the Pittsburgh Foundation, we were able to organize fundraisers for the day. Proceeds were allocated to some of Christian's favorite organizations, including Young Adult Survivors United (YASU). The support gave hope to young adults and their family members facing life-changing cancer diagnoses.

(pittsburghfoundation.org/christiancochran)

Christian's legacy of inclusivity, positivity, and love continued to influence others. Tributes came pouring in for a long time after his passing. Jim Scriven, the Pine-Richland musical director (2015–2016), wrote the following in a letter to honor Christian's legacy within the Pine-Richland Theater Program:

Christian was a ray of sunshine during every rehearsal, and truly embodied the kindness and camaraderie that permeated through the Pine-Richland musical experience every year.

Joy: He brought joy to the lives of those he was around every day. His characters in the shows brought joy to those who were lucky enough to see him perform. He created joy even during moments when it felt like things may not work out. Every single evening you could count on walking away from that auditorium feeling joy when you were around Christian.

In September 2023, a snapshot captured the arrival of new students in the Pine Richland High School parking lot, marking the first day of their educational journey. The photo was sent by Margee Rottinghaus and it showed an empty parking space filled with chalk writing on the tarmac. At the bottom right of the image, someone had written *what's good about today*—C. C. Margee commented that we probably knew whose parking space that was and that she couldn't think of a better way to start the school year—with Christian's inspirational message.

I love how those colorful words mirror the endless skies.

# Cultivating a Gratitude Mindset

"A noble person is mindful and thankful for the favors he receives from others "–The Buddha (Schenck, 2011, para 1)

Gratitude is a term we broadly use, but do we truly consider the significant impact of gratitude on our lives? Recent research indicates the undeniable benefits of living a grateful life. Most studies show an association between gratitude and a person's general sense of well-being. Some of these studies were based on gratitude letter writing: It has been found that such writing refocuses a person's words away from toxic emotions (such as envy or resentment) to more soothing emotions (such as blessings).

One of the leading researchers in this field is the psychologist Dr. Martin E. P. Seligman from the University of Pennsylvania. He led a study where 411 people took part in various positive psychology interventions. One of their assignments was to write a letter of gratitude to someone in their lives (someone from a past memory) who never received a formal thank you letter from them for something they did. They had to properly thank this person and personally deliver the letter to them. It was found that the assignment was associated with a general increase in happiness, which exhibited higher scores: Even more noteworthy was the fact that this action transformed their lives for months afterward. It furthermore exhibited higher scores on the impact scale than the other interventions of the study's assignments (Harvard Health Publishing, 2021, para 7).

There are always exceptions to the rule: Some studies have found a neutral correlation to offering a tangible note or expression of gratitude, but these were mostly aligned with varying emotional maturity levels in different age groups. The point is that many respondents find a positive relation after gratitude expression! The primary benefit of having a gratitude mindset is that it shifts the focus away from what is *lacking* in life to what is *present* in one's life. Although refocusing such a mindset may feel a bit contrived initially, it does become more natural with regular practice.

Gratitude and mindfulness open up changed perspectives. It's furthermore a deliberate choice to not only focus on one aspect, but to see the negative, the positive, and the neutral in every situation. You observe yourself, others, and the world with a keen curiosity and through nonjudgmental eyes. Most importantly, you accept what is there. That's how we reframe gratitude—by mindfully observing the reality, slowing down, and finding acceptance. That's how we cultivate a gratitude mindset.

Many of us have distorted views of our realities because we compete, race, compare, and lose sight of the truth on our journeys. Some focus only on the negatives making their lives mired in darkness and negativity. Others oppose this by blissfully ignoring the darker moments and living a "fake" positivity. Both these approaches deny us our rightful reality in the here and now. Instead, a more mindful approach takes out all judgment, observes with full awareness, simply accepts what is there, and reflects on the things to be grateful for—whether they are dark, light, or neutral.

Of course, this reflection has to be authentic, as gratitude cannot be faked. You cannot deceive your mind—it knows better than you, and if you ignore the truth, the mind finds its way around all the busyness that you cram into it. Eventually, that overwhelms and simply spirals you back into a state of despair. Gratitude is a learned skill. It's a deliberate choice to slow down and observe the truth with humility. It's a skill that can be strengthened and developed with regular practice.

The word is derived from the Latin *gratia* which translates as grace/graciousness. This gracefulness implies a humble acceptance of all the things that are in our lives whether we perceive them as favorable or not/wanted or unwanted. The biggest benefit of this approach is that it helps us to connect to a higher power. That higher power could have a different meaning for all of us: It could be a deity, nature, or other people. Still, the benefits of gratitude are consistently associated with greater joy, positive emotions, relishing experiences in a joyful manner, improved relationships, enhanced well-being, and calmly dealing with adversity.

# The Path of Positivity

Positivity is a three-dimensional concept that implies emotions, thoughts, and behaviors. Positive emotions are often felt through joy, contentment, and enthusiasm. Christian embodied all of these. Through practicing random acts of kindness, following a healthy lifestyle, and doing good deeds for society, he shared his optimism for life. Having an optimistic outlook on life has many advantages. The Buddhist saying that suggests our actions are the results of our thoughts comes to mind here. Buddha's followers believe that positivity is not merely a result of thinking in a positive way, but actively taking part in positive behaviors. In this way, we can create a life of optimism by applying our positive intentions to our habits and our actions. Actively engaging in such a way leads to enhanced positivity, setting us up for more meaningful connections.

Such commitment to authentic positivity is closely related to our sense of self-worth and gratitude. Being grateful for what we have, who we have in our lives, and what brings us joy all cultivates a path of positivity. Christian's example of positivity and gratefulness has set the course for others to follow. He wrote a verse from the Holy Bible in his backpack—as if to walk with him on his journey. It was the following verse from Psalm 23:

> The Lord is my Shepherd.
>
> I shall not want.
>
> He makes me to lie down in green pastures.
>
> He leads me in the still waters.
>
> He restores my soul.
>
> He leads me in the paths of righteousness for His name's sake.
>
> Yes, as I walk through the valley of the shadow of death, I will fear no evil, for you are with me.

Christian never preached his spiritual ways; he lived them. He embraced all and made them his own in his unique way of expressing kindness and love. His positive approach to life paved the way for meaningful relationships. The tributes came pouring in after his passing—some in words, some in art form, some through music. There were too many to share with you in this book, but I would like to highlight a few to illustrate the impact of Christian's authenticity.

## *Touched by Christian's Legacy*

Tributes from Christian's network of friends from his student years spoke eloquently of his unique character, mostly commenting on his kind and genuine nature. When reading through these, it becomes clear how Christian never enforced these concepts on anybody. He merely lived his life in *his* authentic way, and in the way that intuitively felt right to *him*. Through his persuasive example, he quietly set the trajectory for others to follow. What follows are several of these tributes, most of which take the form of a letter sent to our family. To begin with, one of his friends sent us a letter, sharing some of the following inspirational moments with Christian:

> Christian really touched so many people. I think that's something a lot of people don't think about when someone passes. A lot of times, people pay attention to their successes or things of that nature and, although Christian was incredibly successful as well, that's not what I think most people will remember him for. I know I will remember him for his kindness and ability to really brighten a room. I never saw Christian without a smile on his face.
>
> Mr Cochran, please know how special Christian was to so many people. He always said such wonderful things about your family. I remember years ago, we were sitting at lunch together and your daughter was in a car accident, I believe, and Christian had just received the news. I have never met someone so devoted to his family and I really admired that about him.

Another friend from his college years had this to say:

> His willingness to share parts of himself so quickly and openly with others made talking to him feel safe and fun. Years later, he started a conga line with a friend while students were evacuated from a residence hall after a fire. It was 3 a.m., we were tired, bored, and worried—yet Christian still got a line going. He consistently found ways to uplift others. I'll never forget how nice it was to just be around him: a laugh or smile was always guaranteed.

John Appolonia wrote to us, stressing some words in the note:

> Though you all certainly witnessed it for yourselves, Christian left such a positive impression on every person who had the pleasure of meeting him. He was able to reach people in many ways with his wit, his energy, his intelligence, his originality, his artistic talents, and his sincere kindness and compassion for others. All of these enabled him to cultivate meaningful connections with people from all walks of life. His legacy will be lasting for so many as a result.

Here is a letter from Emma Russek:

> When I first got to college, I was in a very dark and lonely place. Then I met Christian. He immediately accepted me for who I was. He took me under his wing, and accepted me into his group of friends. I have never in my life met someone as funny and kind as Christian. He never failed to make me laugh. He completely changed my perspective on life, teaching me to be grateful for the little things and to find humor in everything.

One of his childhood friends' parents, Gregg Broujos, wrote these words to us:

> Christian's mantra that you mentioned at the funeral, what's good about today, completely sums up Christian's beautiful spirit and unselfish nature. And with your permission, our family is using it every day as a type of guide rail for life. His mantra has completely changed my life. I'm not generally a

negative person, but when I do have a negative episode, I stop; I think about Christian, I think about his mantra, and I immediately become less negative. When I think about Christian—which is often—I can feel his kindness surround me. And his mantra really does help me every day to be a kinder, gentler person. Just think: If all the people he has touched, and all the people who didn't know him (but who hear his story), can be that much less negative, then truly, what a wonderful world is being created.

Here is a supportive letter from our friend, Kristin:

> I think about him in all his plays, playing the cymbals in the band, his space podcast, trying his hand at the sport his father loved—wrestling—when he was a little boy, and that beautiful face that filled the big screen in the Batman movie!
>
> His love of random acts of kindness, his mantra of what's good about today, and his desire to make other people feel special and happy even on his most difficult days—these will be his legacy that will forever change the world. His short life truly made this world a better place. I believe the legacies he left in this world will eventually not only affect the people he knew, but the entire universe. He put out such a strong spirit of energy, positivity, and love into the universe that it will eventually touch everyone.

Next, a letter by Stacy Dennison:

> I have known Christian since he was in kindergarten class with my daughter. They grew up on the same street and were in many musicals together. Christian was always full of life and kindness.
>
> Christian's celebration of his life was a true testimony to just how far and wide his light shines. There were people from different backgrounds, ethnicities, religions, and ages from children to the elderly who paid respect and celebrated the true light he was (and is) when we learned of his passing.

> If there is a modern version of a saint or one who walked in the footsteps of Jesus—it was Christian. I truly believe his impact on me and so many others has come at a time when so many are hurting and have forgotten what's good about today.

Moving on, I would like to share with you a letter from Melissa, dated October 10th, 2020.

This is a letter from the very first nurse we met on the first day of chemotherapy at Hillman Cancer Center. She remained one of Christian's nurses throughout his year of treatment there. It was Wednesday, September 8th, 2020. Danielle took him to chemo that day because of COVID-19 when only one parent could attend. When we embarked on this first step of our long life-changing journey, our neighbors had tied sparkling dark green balloons in the shape of stars throughout our neighborhood. They wanted to show their love and support for Christian and our family on his first day of chemotherapy.

> I've written this letter multiple times, edited it, rewrote the whole thing, and then started all over again. I couldn't figure out why I struggled with finishing this letter to a point that satisfied me. I finally realized it was because Christian's impact was beyond words. His presence was so big, so bright, so faithful, that there are no words or descriptions that can do him justice. His impact was so much more. My thoughts and words will only be able to convey a fraction of Christian's impact.
>
> I've always been a faithful person. Working in oncology, my faith is sometimes the only thing that can get me through the most difficult days. Christian embodied faith more than anyone that I have ever witnessed. I could feel the presence of God with each and every encounter I was privileged to have spent with him.
>
> Christian's positivity was so strong and honestly beyond reason. If there was ever a person who had every right to be angry, mad, and/or negative, it would have been Christian. Instead, he was continuously positive through each and every day. He had the ability to make everyone he met feel special. He made

everyone realize that their own blessings were bigger and more numerous than they believed.

Christian's light was so incredibly bright and warm. You could not help but be drawn to him and the light he exuded. His faith, positivity, and light had an impact on each individual he met. He made every person feel special. If they did not feel blessed before meeting Christian, they absolutely felt blessed after.

He would always ask how my day was, how my family was, and how life was—with such pure honesty. He taught me that even on my roughest day, I could and should show concern and kindness to others because their day could be worse.

It was truly an honor, privilege, and a blessing to have been graced with being in Christian's amazing presence. It was a gift that I will forever remember.

Now, here is a letter Alexa Smith sent to our family:

Christian was one of the first people to make me okay with being at college. At the time, I struggled with immense social anxiety. I feared being anywhere other than my childhood home because I always felt like the world around me was judging me for one reason or another. I became best friends with Christian's roommate, and due to issues with my own roommate, I started spending a lot of time in Christian's dorm room.

Every time I knocked on the door seeking a quiet place to study or just relax, Christian would greet me without questioning a thing. It did not matter if it was the first time I knocked that day or the fifth time. The genuine excitement behind him saying, "Smitty!" every time I stepped into his room was the warmth and reassurance I needed to know I would never be a bother and was always welcome. Christian even started referring to me as his "honorary roommate." He never complained about my presence, and he accepted me exactly as I was. Christian's smile, unconditional kindness, and warm personality brought so much comfort and light to my days at college.

Christian reminded me of the value of selfless acts. His message warmed my heart and made my day.

Here is a touching letter from Nurse Alison Searight:

> I cannot think of a more perfect modern-day example of a saint than Christian himself.
>
> My experience with your wonderful family, and Christian, of course, bring both fond and sad memories. I remember August 26th, 2020 like it was yesterday. I had only been working at the unit for about two weeks when Bonnie and I were assigned to be Christian's nurses. I remember how nervous I was at the sheer thought of being responsible for people's lives. To this day, it sometimes remains a little scary. I guess Christian could sense my nervous energy, but from the second I made eye contact with those big beautiful brown eyes, my fears just melted away. We started with small talk, the usual "Where are you from" and all that, and the second I found out we both were thespians, the rest was history. I found myself just hanging out in Christian's room when I had a few spare minutes. Just his physical presence gave me such a sense of security; it's almost as if Christian would ground me again when the world was spinning out of control. It didn't even matter what the conversation topic was, Christian was just so damn easy to talk to, it was almost intoxicating. His little jokes were my favorite.
>
> Then that horrible day came. That gut-wrenching news arrived confirming all of our worst fears. Bonnie and I knew how bad it was before Dr. Humar and his team came in to tell everyone. I cried alone in the supply room just praying that no one would walk in so I didn't have to say the C word out loud: cholangiocarcinoma.
>
> I remember composing myself, and as soon as the doctors were out of that room, Bonnie and I were in. In nursing school, they

never teach you how to deal with these kinds of situations. As a nurse, I'm supposed to fix and save people, but I didn't know how to help Christian. What happened next I will never forget. I remember sitting at the foot of Christian's bed, just trying to think of something positive to say, when your angel son grabbed my hand and just said, "Have you gotten a break today?" In that insane moment of pure life-altering terror that was leaving everyone (including myself) speechless, Christian wanted to make sure I had gotten something to eat. I just remembered mumbling back through tears and snot running down my face, "No." His perfect snappy comeback was, "Well Alli, you know nurses need to eat too." So I did just that.

I'm now a little over a year into my nursing career. I'm still on 11 North, the abdominal transplant unit, and I'm actually a charge nurse now. I grew into my role as a nurse because of Christian. I am so thankful to have gotten a small glimpse of his extraordinary life. Christian helped me to gain confidence in myself and my abilities as a nurse to care for those at their absolute worst. I will always carry that memory of Christian with me for the rest of my life. And thanks to him, I now make a conscious effort to ensure I have a break during my long days because "Nurses need to eat too."

Every time I read Alison's tribute, I get a lump in my throat. I literally see my son, lovingly holding her hand, and engaging with sincere concern to help her face her deep emotional turmoil: Simply focus on nurturing your body. Don't resist the flow. Nurturing your body will ultimately nurture your soul.

An old friend of mine who lives about a 10-hour car drive away recently made contact with me after a long silence stretching back to our college days. We did have occasional phone chats over the years, and I knew he was going through multiple life challenges like much of the world, but it had still been some time since we spoke at length.

His name is Dan, and he knew that Christian had been sick over the previous months. Dan was kind enough to send small gifts to Christian, including that pair of custom-made Nike shoes I mentioned back in Chapter 2 to remind him that *he does not walk alone*. About 30 days before Christian's passing, I felt compelled to tell Dan that Christian had about 30 days left on this Earth, and was deteriorating very quickly. When I told him this news, Dan dropped everything and drove from Chattanooga, TN to Pittsburgh, PA.

I didn't ask Dan to come or even try to give him the impression that I needed him to be there. He just seemed to know. This is the thing about those who understand where they stand in life. Dan had never even met Christian. He knew that Christian had something very special to offer this Earth, and he wanted to see Christian in the living, being alive: Christian at home, in a bed in the living room surrounded by his family.

Dan arrived sometime in the afternoon and knocked on the front door. When he walked in, he immediately went straight to Christian without hesitation and held his hand. They were whispering. Dan said, "I was just amazed at how much light was in his eyes; he was comforting me with his voice." Christian said to Dan, "Can I ask you a favor?" He said "Yes" to that amazing question, and Christian said, "Can you be there for my Dad?" Dan responded, "Absolutely," to which Christian responded, "He's going to need you."

This is just another example of how Christian was thinking of his family in the midst of his own suffering. The meeting between them had a profound impact on Dan's life, who has not only continued to travel and tell Christian's story in different states and at different dance festivals but has also set up stands and simply shared Christian's message of *what's good about today*. He has been handing out *WGAT* stickers, shirts, and wristbands. This has had countless ripple effects on so many lives.

I'd now like to share a letter to the family from Melinda Bachini, one of the few long-term survivors in the world of cholangiocarcinoma:

I have attempted to start this letter so many times over the last few months since Christian's passing. Unfortunately, his passing hit much too close to my heart, as I have also lost a young son and know the heartache of losing a child.

I remember when I first heard about Christian's diagnosis of cholangiocarcinoma from his aunt and uncle, Bridget and David. I was heartbroken and immediately felt a connection to him, because I had just lost my 24-year-old son earlier that year. I wanted to find a way to save him and let him be a miracle in surviving the disease. I knew from the way David and Bridget talked about Christian that he was something special. I went to Christian's website, looked at his pictures, and read about him. His personality shined through the screen. I soon realized how right I was when I met Christian via our Zoom call.

As a 12-year survivor of stage 4 cholangiocarcinoma, I suffer from a great deal of survivor guilt. It especially hits me hard when talking to someone as young, vibrant, and remarkable as Christian. I don't fully understand why I am still alive when so many others are not. I feel strongly about helping others diagnosed with this cancer to the best of my ability. But even with my strong faith, I can still feel the survivor guilt. My survivor guilt is where Christian made the difference to me and touched my life.

While talking to him in the Zoom call, he made me feel comforted—something I try to do for other patients. He was so happy for me. He was delighted that I had survived and was here to be a mother to my children. He told me that it was vital for me to be here for them, and he looked lovingly at both you and Danielle—his parents. He was grateful that I took the time to meet with him and answer questions for him. He told me that I gave him hope. I started that call, thinking I was going to help Christian and his family, but in reality, Christian helped me resolve some of my survivor guilt and look at it from a different perspective. I think of Christian all the time, of the optimism he eluded that day, and of how much he touched me as a mother. I will never forget this. I can still see his smiling face.

I am blessed to have known Christian for a brief moment.

A letter arrived from Dr. Mark Yarchoan, MD/Assistant Professor, Division of GI Malignancies; Sidney Kimmel Comprehensive Cancer Center; Johns Hopkins, Baltimore, MD. As an oncologist at Johns Hopkins, he was involved as one of the many caregivers and medical personnel of Christian. His words are as follows:

I'm sure that you've heard from many already that this young gentleman was a truly remarkable person. He was strong and composed while facing a truly terrible situation. Despite knowing him for only a brief period of time, I think about him frequently. I care for many patients with this cancer, and to this day I do not understand why some people get this terrible cancer, and why some patients have remarkable responses to treatment, and why other patients like Christian do not seem to respond to treatments.

Christian once said that he felt his diagnosis would prevent someone else from getting this terrible diagnosis, and I often think that Christian had more clarity about what was happening than those of us who were caring for him.

When he passed, leftover chemotherapy pills were sent to my home address (these are exceedingly expensive, and they are very useful for cancer research or for patients who do not have insurance). Somebody stole the package from my doorstep, but remarkably, this person returned the package with a note apologizing and explaining that upon realizing the package contained medicine, they felt obliged to return it and are working on getting help for addiction. Upon reading this, I felt Christian's guiding spirit already helping others around us.

I hope that one day we will have a cure for this terrible cancer, and that Christian will help us to get a cure.

Here are a few excerpts from a letter from Debe Stadelmyer, a receptionist at Hillman Cancer Institute:

For Christian Cochran —

From day one, when I met Christian, he instantly reminded me of my twin sons. His eyes lit up as I told him. It's a memory of Christian that I will always remember.

He had so much going for him, especially his faith. He always arrived asking how I was doing instead of talking about himself.

I remember riding in the elevator with him and telling him that if it's not working, we need to kneel down. He looked at me and said, "You remind me of my mother." Oh my, his faith was so strong, even on his not-so-great days.

He left us with an everlasting impression of how we all need to be like him and value faith as an everlasting gift from God. I miss him and know God has taken a wonderful strong young man to help out in heaven.

The Jochem family shared another touching letter with our family, as follows:

He was always smiling and he amazingly carried these traits throughout his illness despite the horrific treatments and pain he had to endure.

During his long battle with the disease, we came by weekly to pray and walk the dogs, and he was always filled with gratitude and concern about us. And he always had a smile on his face! His strong faith and grace throughout this journey certainly strengthened my faith: It was truly unbelievable to witness.

We also received a letter from a woman who prefers to remain anonymous but who was greatly moved by Christian's story. This is what she wrote:

Dear Cochran family,

This letter may come as a surprise to you, so let me introduce myself first. I'm a writer and have to do extensive research for my nonfiction books. On one occasion, while researching for a book based on the theme of lives that made a significant impact on others, I stumbled upon your beloved son's website. I ventured deeper into the outpour of tributes on the page and became intensely aware of the deep admiration and respect he attracted throughout his life from others.

It didn't stop there. Something compelled me to find out more about this unknown young man I'd read about in various online publications. His mantra—what's good about today—became a guiding star on my own journey. I could not imagine the devastating loss and suffering your family must have endured. The fact that despite all of this, Christian guided you as a family—as well as so many other people out there—to follow his incredibly inspirational mantra within this suffering world and the thing we call living, remains exceptional.

And then I had a profound experience that I'd like to share. My daughter recently had to do an emergency MRI scan after concerns were raised by a previous brain scan. We had to rule out any benign tumors or similar diseases that affect the white matter of the brain. She is in her late 20s and we were extremely concerned.

I told her about Christian's mantra and his story in an attempt to not only settle my own fears, but to encourage her to focus on the path that is laid out for us and showing her that there is always something to be grateful for: her supportive family.

My daughter is highly claustrophobic and the second MRI required a 30-minute scan. This added to her fears. She asked me to stay with her during the procedure to help her stay calm. Naturally, I appeared calm—as any mother would do to help her child—but deep within, my heart was close to breaking point. The uncertainty of the outcome of that scan was the pinnacle of all my lifelong fears.

I sat beside her as she glided into that tunnel, entering the longest 30 minutes of my entire life. I had to keep my eyes open so that I could immediately respond on her demand, if needed. My whole body was trembling in that eternity. Then I heard Christian's voice. It sounded like a "dancing" voice—a positively lively voice—and in his caring way, he said to me, "Everything will be okay." I have never heard his voice, but I can tell you that what I heard in that closed room with only my vulnerable daughter, my fearful self, and the MRI sounds slowly ticking the time away—was a young yet wise voice. And it calmed me down.

My body stopped shaking. My daughter lay still, unnerved by what was happening, and we walked out of that room both feeling relieved and undaunted by the imminent outcome. In your loving son's soothing embrace, we found tranquility and the strength to face what we had to face.

My daughter is still with me, and after this experience, I became increasingly aware of the devastation of your loss and how you must cry against a world that doesn't always value life. Even though I have never met him in person, he lives within my heart now. I will show my respect to your family and your beloved child when I am able to travel to his birthplace, and place my gratitude at the feet of his memorial garden.

Thank you for making a difference in this world, through Christian, and a life well lived.

David Gautreau, the Louisiana-based musician, wrote a song about Christian and his inspirational mantra, *what's good about today*. He continues to perform it all over the US. David never knew Christian personally but heard about his remarkable story from a relative who used to be Christian's teacher in elementary school. The life story she relayed to David inspired him deeply. He was mostly inspired by Christian's loving, brave, and faithful response to his terminal illness as well as his mantra to find the *good* in every day to guide his life and all those whose lives he touched.

To honor Christian he said, "The faith and determination they [the family] have in sharing Christian's message is making a difference in this hurting world. Christian and his powerful story is truly a blessing to all" (Long, 2023, para 5). He furthermore hoped that his song would provide courage, faith, strength, and healing to listeners.

The song can be found on most music platforms including ReverbNation, Spotify, and Apple Music. (bit.ly/3QrDOz2)

Katie, a friend of Christian from college, shared details about a profound experience relating to him, as follows:

> A couple of months ago, I was on a long reflective drive alone. It was really emotional for me, especially while reliving some of my memories with Christian. My thoughts spiraled into ways that overwhelmed me with feelings of guilt. I reflected on how I could have been better.
>
> Suddenly, I felt all the negativity wash away in a way that I have never experienced before, and I was left with a sense of true peace. I began to cry, and then the alarm for the seat next to me went off: the one that tells a passenger to fasten their seat belt because it senses weight. This happened three hours into the drive without any prior alarm going off.
>
> I haven't shared this with anyone because I felt it would be ridiculous to assume Christian would be with me when he has so many loved ones who need him with them. But after some time to process what happened, I thought it was important to share this incident with you.
>
> It has moved me deeply and changed my perspective on spirituality in a way I never thought possible. (I wasn't raised in a religious home.)

I think that Will Newell, who was among several close friends of Christian, summed up the essence of Christian's uniqueness very well in his tribute. I would like to share some powerful excerpts from his letter below:

> When I think of what Christian meant to me as a friend, and still means to me today, I think of how he made me feel.
>
> I felt that, no matter where our lives took us—to college, to work, to new relationships, and new chapters in life—Christian would always be there, pulling us back together with the people we loved.
>
> I felt we could relate—deeply, vulnerably, and without judgment.

By now, Christian's friends have shared hundreds of memories like this with one another. How did each of us feel such a deep connection with him? The answer, I think, is that Christian saw and cherished what was best in each of us. And he told us what he saw.

He was so generous in his love that he saw beautiful qualities in all of his friends. And in doing so, he helped us to see the best qualities in ourselves. Christian was so warm, empathetic, funny, and intellectually curious that we could not help but believe him when he said he saw these traits in us.

I was so proud to call Christian my friend. I felt that, because he had chosen to be my friend, there must be something special about me: something worth loving.

Christian told his friends he loved them so often that we (in good humor) gave him a hard time for it. It was a telltale sign that he was having fun. But Christian said he loved me in our most sober moments, too, like when we first spoke after his diagnosis. In this, Christian was utterly unique. It's too rare that we say we love each other. It's almost unheard of among young men and boys. Therefore, the first thing I will remember whenever I think of Christian is his unabashed love. Christian's love is his most enduring, Christ-like gift to us.

We should share it generously.

[The author took the liberty of adjusting the individual tributes for readability.]

Just imagine the impact of making others *feel* differently... and thus connecting on such a profound level of trust. Have you made someone feel special today? Will's characterization of what Christian meant to him as a friend—and why—compelled me to strive to touch others' lives the way Christian did.

Christian's favorite Bible verse is Luke 21:1–4. Not many people pay attention to this unusual verse, but it meant so much to Christian. His nature of giving love and kindness to others relates very well with the words of Christ because when you read the verse, it's about giving *all* of yourself to others—not merely giving halfheartedly. It reads as follows:

> The Widow's Offering:
>
> As Jesus looked up, He saw the rich putting their gifts into the temple treasury. He also saw a poor widow put in two very small copper coins. "Truly I tell you," He said, "This poor widow has put in more than all the others. All these people gave their gifts out of their wealth; but she out of her poverty put in all she had to live on."

For me, this is such a strong reminder of what Christian felt was important. It remains a powerful reminder to us that we must give to those who are in need and put all of ourselves out there for others.

In Christian's application for graduate school, he reflected on "the peculiar opportunity to examine my life in an objective view." Notwithstanding the aggressively destructive nature of this "opportunity," he maintained the notion of facing it with positivity. To me, it's admirable that he did not shy away from his related emotions. Instead, he embraced his vulnerability to redefine his strength and purpose:

> I do not intend to imply that cancer has given me some sort of new sense of self, but rather that it has allowed me to feel vulnerable and evaluate what is important to me. –Christian Cochran

# Conclusion

*Be the change you want to see in the world.* –Anonymous

On the day of Christian's passing, the street outside our home was lined with green lights all the way down. Christian's favorite color was green: All the lights were green... We opened our door and saw this incredible gesture of respect and heartwarming love as it poured out from the neighborhood. The people who showed up in front of our house were praying and showing their love for our heartbroken family and beloved Christian. I will never forget that sight. Most of those lights still line our street as a beautiful reminder of how many lives our beautiful boy has touched.

Christian lived his life purposefully to make a change. He did this in his compassionately generous way. He never imposed his view—he subtly illustrated his beliefs through his example. And that example is what we follow. As has been said, his heart was truly bigger than his entire body. He left a legacy of love that I believe will change the world.

The St. Stanislaus Kostka Church in the Strip District dedicated a memorial garden to Christian in 2022. They follow the tradition of the Pantheon in Rome to shower its parishioners with rose petals from the center of its ceiling during some celebratory and religious events. This symbolizes the showering down of God's gifts. During the opening ceremony of the memorial garden, the showering of yellow rose petals symbolized Christian's care and love from heaven, much like a ray of sunshine on your shoulder. (The same pattern of petal showering was followed during Christian's memorial service, the previous year, symbolizing God's gifts of love.)

The prayer garden is a lasting reminder of Christian's positive outlook on life and his courageous battle with a terminal illness. He leaves a visible legacy for all who pass this historic church. The garden's centerpiece is a white stone angel (a replica of an antique Italian statue) surrounded by green plants, lights, and a water feature. All of these are elements that echo Christian's existence: his love of the Earth, his love for the color green, being a beacon of light, his angelic spirit, and his sincere devotion to navigating the flow of life and not resisting its predestined path.

The plaque is inscribed with his bio—a short introduction on how he dedicated his life to finding joy in every moment, his humble ways, and how he generously showered all with his boundless kindness. The inscription reads: *With God in our hearts, like Christian, we may create ripples of love and shimmers of light everywhere we journey.* A single moment spent in front of this garden creates quietude and a deep admiration for Christian's resilience. Whenever we go to visit the site, we are reminded of his powerful mantra, *what's good about today?* We are reminded of his empathy when all he wanted was for others (including his beloved family) not to suffer.

We still grieve; we all grieve in our individual ways. There is no right or wrong way to grieve. We learn from others and we let go of what may not work for us. But one thing that I have learned from grief is that it never goes away. It only softens with time and acceptance. Perhaps we should understand from this lesson that we cannot fight the overwhelming emotions accompanying our grief. We can merely "live" them, and make them ours in a way that carries us through the inevitable darker days.

Christian not only remains in our hearts forever, but through his love for others, he has left us with visible signs all over the world of lasting physical connection and collective power: the power of nonresistance. The power of kindness and healing. The power of holding each other and never letting go. The power of unconditional caring. The power of gratitude, of a positive mind, and of generosity. And most of all, the power of unconditional love. Christian trusted God's plan, he trusted the river's flow, and he carried his burden with dignity, grace, and humility. I reiterate: When he gave his last breath to this earthly sphere, Dr. Zaida held the moment with our family in the living room of our house and said, "Christian showed us how to live—and how to die."

If someone had to ask you how you want to be remembered after death, what would you say to them? What would you truthfully *like* to say? I think the answer to such a question sums up our core principles in life. It proves the way we live and conduct ourselves—subconsciously—because it inherently drives our actions.

Christian trusted his family. His family trusted the ways of the universe and its journey. How beautiful that Christian never asked for credibility; he simply accepted the other person's requests. He trusted humanity. He trusted the good of mankind. He trusted love. Perhaps this is our main lesson: to start trusting, to reconnect, to be there—not only for ourselves but also for others. Isn't this what the world needs right now? To slow down, to have compassion, to show love, and to trust.

One reason why regret holds such power is that we find ourselves trapped in the past more often than not. Instead of embracing the present, we spend our days dwelling on yesterday. We replay scenarios, wondering what we could or should have done differently, and we endlessly ruminate on how others have wronged us. In this cycle, we become so consumed by the past that we completely miss out on the wonders unfolding before us in the here and now.

Furthermore, by fixating on the future, we inadvertently skip over the present moment, only to later regret our oversight. Little do we realize that the true power, joy, rewards, connection, and love lie within the present. It is the only reality, for our fears of the future and regrets of the past are nothing but diluted perceptions. Happiness and gratitude reside in embracing the present moment, in being fully present. Christian was always fully present, every day.

Life can be distressing. We merely have to look at the news to understand that people have forgotten the concepts of love and compassion. How does the younger generation aim to change this? If they can follow Christian's example, perhaps the ripple effect of their outcry will touch humanity. I firmly believe the world may change for the better if we approach life positively, not negatively. The world is exposing our youth to so many horrors, but at least we can guide them to face it positively and actively make a change; navigating the natural flow of life instead of resisting it. Perhaps when we give and share our love more generously, things will improve. Perhaps we needed a modern-day saint—like Christian—to set the example for the rest of us to follow. Let's follow his guidance and find the *good* in every moment.

"Family means love and hope." –Christian Cochran

*** 

If you have found this book useful, do share the delightful and inspirational moments with others. Our family would be grateful if you left a sincere review that could encourage others to learn more about Christian's inspirational life.

# References

American Cancer Society. (n.d.). *Bile duct cancer survival rates - cholangiocarcinoma survival rates*. Cancer. https://www.cancer.org/cancer/types/bile-duct-cancer/detection-diagnosis-staging/survival-by-stage.html

Biscuit People. (2017, November 10). *Pizzelle: Traditional biscuit with a long history*. https://www.biscuitpeople.com/magazine/post/pizzelle-traditional-biscuit

Bodhipaksa. (n.d.). *"What you think you create, what you feel you attract, what you imagine you become"*. Fakebuddhaquotes. https://fakebuddhaquotes.com/what-you-think-you-create-what-you-feel-you-attract-what-you-imagine-you-become/

BrainyQuote. (n.d.). *Grief quotes*. https://www.brainyquote.com/topics/grief-quotes

Brown, J., & Wong, J. (2017, June 6). *How gratitude changes you and your brain*. Greater Good; The Greater Good Science Center at the University of California, Berkeley. https://greatergood.berkeley.edu/article/item/how_gratitude_changes_you_and_your_brain

CaringBridge. (2022, August 27). *Christian Cochran*. https://www.caringbridge.org/visit/christiancochran

Chmiel, P., Gęca, K., Rawicz-Pruszyński, K., Polkowski, W. P., & Skórzewska, M. (2022). FGFR inhibitors in cholangiocarcinoma—a novel yet primary approach: Where do we stand now and where to head next in targeting this axis? *Cells, 11*(23), 3929. https://doi.org/10.3390/cells11233929

Christian Cochran Foundation. (2021). *Become part of the*. WGAT. https://www.christiancochran.org/

Crossroads Hospice. (2017, July 19). *Understanding end-of-life visions*. https://www.crossroadshospice.com/hospice-palliative-care-blog/2017/july/19/understanding-end-of-life-visions/

Davis, T. (2023). *Positivity: The psychology, definition, and examples*. The Berkeley Well-Being Institute. https://www.berkeleywellbeing.com/positivity.html

Gillette, H., & Gepp, K. (2022, January 28). *Feeling a presence after a loss: Hallucination or vision of grief?* PsychCentral. https://psychcentral.com/health/grief-hallucinations-vision-loss#recap

Goodreads. (n.d.-a). *A quote by Anne Frank*. https://www.goodreads.com/quotes/6483575-dead-people-receive-more-flowers-than-the-living-ones-because

Goodreads. (n.d.-b). *Rumi (Jalal ad-Din Muhammad ar-Rumi) quotes (author of the essential Rumi)*. https://www.goodreads.com/author/quotes/875661.Rumi_Jalal_ad_Din_Muhammad_ar_Rumi_?page=2

Harvard Health Publishing. (2021, August 14). *Giving thanks can make you happier*. https://www.health.harvard.edu/healthbeat/giving-thanks-can-make-you-happier

Hersh, E., & Barlow, B. (2022, April 13). *CAR T-cell therapy: Benefits, risks, outlook*. Healthline. https://www.healthline.com/health/car-t-cell-therapy

Johns Hopkins Medicine. (2021, August 30). *Bile duct cancer (cholangiocarcinoma)*. https://www.hopkinsmedicine.org/health/conditions-and-diseases/bile-duct-cancer-cholangiocarcinoma

Kamp, K. S., Steffen, E. M., Alderson-Day, B., Allen, P., Austad, A., Hayes, J., Larøi, F., Ratcliffe, M., & Sabucedo, P. (2020). Sensory and quasi-sensory experiences of the deceased in bereavement: An interdisciplinary and integrative review. *Schizophrenia Bulletin, 46*(6). https://doi.org/10.1093/schbul/sbaa113

Liles, J. (2021, October 16). *No, Anne Frank did not say "Dead people receive more flowers."* Snopes. https://www.snopes.com/fact-check/anne-frank-flowers-quote/

Long, J. (2023, September). What's good about today - songwriter David Gautreau. *EDIT, EDIT*(EDIT), 20.

Mahadane, R. (2019, November 1). *The philosophy of flow — Taoism*. Medium. https://medium.com/novasemita/the-philosophy-of-flow-taoism-f176f1de2999

Mayo Clinic. (n.d.). *Hydromorphone (oral route) description and brand names*. https://www.mayoclinic.org/drugs-supplements/hydromorphone-oral-route/description/drg-20074171

Mayo Clinic. (2019). *Cholangiocarcinoma (bile duct cancer) - symptoms and causes*. https://www.mayoclinic.org/diseases-conditions/cholangiocarcinoma/symptoms-causes/syc-20352408

Milner, J. (2022, June 6). Strip district church dedicates a garden to a positive parishioner - "What's good about today?" *Pittsburgh Post-Gazette*. https://www.post-gazette.com/life/goodness/2022/06/06/church-dedicates-a-garden-to-a-positive-parishioner-strip-district/stories/202205220176

National Cancer Institute. (2011). *Definition of pemazyre.* Cancer. https://www.cancer.gov/publications/dictionaries/cancer-terms/def/pemazyre

National Library of Medicine. (2020, June 1). *Cholangiocarcinoma: MedlinePlus genetics.* MedlinePlus. https://medlineplus.gov/genetics/condition/cholangiocarcinoma/

O'Toole, W. (2021, March 2). *"Row, row, row your boat" and Tao philosophy.* Inspiring Communities. https://inspiringcommunities.ca/2021/03/02/row-row-row-your-boat-and-tao-philosophy/

Patel, S. (2023, February 27). *How aggressive is bile duct cancer?* Healthline. https://www.healthline.com/health/cancer/how-aggressive-is-bile-duct-cancer#how-fast-does-it-spread

Phillips, J. L. (n.d.). *Origin story: Be the change.* JLP. https://jenniferlphillips.com/blog/2021/2/24/origin-story-be-the-change

Piper, E. (2023). *History of the pizzelle - the world's oldest cookie.* Unique Dining. https://www.udecatering.com/catering-blog/2018/4/19/history-of-the-pizzelle-the-worlds-oldest-cookie

Quotefancy. (n.d.-a). *Bruce Lee quote.* https://quotefancy.com/quote/4046/Bruce-Lee-Do-not-pray-for-an-easy-life-pray-for-the-strength-to-endure-a-difficult-one

Quotefancy. (n.d.-b). *Henry van Dyke quote.* https://quotefancy.com/quote/1047623/Henry-van-Dyke-Every-house-where-love-abides-And-friendship-is-a-guest-Is-surely-home-and

Quotefancy. (2024). *Anne Frank quotes.* https://quotefancy.com/anne-frank-quotes

Schenck, L. K. (2011, November 23). *Mindfulness & gratitude.* Mindfulness Muse. https://www.mindfulnessmuse.com/mindfulness-exercises/mindfulness-gratitude

Sharpe, R. (2020, September 17). *100+ inspiring Buddha quotes on life and meditation.* Declutter the Mind. https://declutterthemind.com/blog/buddha-quotes/

ShavingFoam. (2020, September 13). *22 years old with cholangiocarcinoma.* Reddit. https://www.reddit.com/r/cancer/comments/irytos/22_years_old_with_cholangiocarcinoma/

Simon, S. (2020, April 2). *FDA approves pemazyre (pemigatinib) for bile duct cancer.* American Cancer Society. https://www.cancer.org/cancer/latest-news/fda-approves-pemazyre-pemigatinib-for-bile-duct-cancer.html

Singh, H. N. (2024, February 23). *Tao te Ching – verse 33 – knowing others is intelligence; knowing yourself is true wisdom.* Harinam and Healing Heart Center. https://www.harinam.com/tao-te-ching-verse-33-knowing-others-is-intelligence-knowing-yourself-is-true-wisdom-2/

Tearle, O. (2021, July 6). *The meaning and origins of "we are such stuff as dreams are made on."* Interesting Literature. https://interestingliterature.com/2021/07/tempest-such-stuff-dreams-made-on-meaning-analysis/

Tzu, L. (2001). *Tao teh Ching* (J. Legge, Trans.). Axiom Publishing.

Uecker, D. J. (2019, July 10). *Entrainment: How life is compelling us to heal.* BioSoul Integration Center. https://www.biosoulintegration.com/law-of-entrainment/

Volpe, L. (2016, December 31). *Pizzelle! Reliving the past through the world's most ancient cookie.* Medium. https://blog.ememory.it/pizzelle-reliving-the-past-through-the-worlds-most-ancient-cookie-23c15dd577bb

Wikipedia. (2022, May 2). *Vinegar tasters.* https://en.wikipedia.org/wiki/Vinegar_tasters

Wikipedia. (2023a, January 20). *Pizzelle.* https://en.wikipedia.org/wiki/Pizzelle

Wikipedia. (2023b, August 4). *The Tao of Pooh.* https://en.wikipedia.org/wiki/The_Tao_of_Pooh

Wikipedia. (2024, March 3). *Taoism and death.* https://en.wikipedia.org/wiki/Taoism_and_death

Williams, R. (2022, October 24). *The oak tree poem by John Ray Ryder Jr.* Lifeism. https://lifeism.co/the-oak-tree-poem

Printed in the USA
CPSIA information can be obtained
at www.ICGtesting.com
CBHW030102220624
10460CB00001B/1

9 798218 432867